Jane McLoughlin was educated at several schools in England and went to university in Ireland. She is former industrial editor and women's editor of the *Guardian* and author of *The Demographic Revolution*, *Up and Running: Women in Business* (Virago, 1992) and the thriller *Coincidence* (also published by Virago, 1992). She lives in Somerset.

On the Death of a Parent

edited by

Jane McLoughlin

Published by VIRAGO PRESS Limited October 1994
20 Vauxhall Bridge Road, London SW1V 2SA

Reprinted 1995

A CIP catalogue record for this book is available
from the British Library

Typeset by M Rules
Printed and bound in Great Britain by
Mackays of Chatham PLC, Chatham, Kent

CONTENTS

JANE MCLOUGHLIN

Introduction

My father and I were in the snake house at London Zoo. He was the only man who would ever come with me to the snake house. He was generally a brave man. He had been on the raid to St Nazaire; he had been behind enemy lines in the Balkans. He did not fear death. He asked me to 'help him out' when the time came. He thought he had a brain tumour. He was awaiting the results of tests. If so, he was definite: he wanted to die before he became irrational, or lost control and dignity.

It wasn't a brain tumour. His death came ten years later, from lung cancer. And I was glad when he died.

I went to visit him unexpectedly in the hospital after an operation to remove part of his lung. He was out of the ward when I came. I waited by his bed. A group of frail old men shuffled past a window. I wanted to weep for those poor helpless old men like battered puppets children had tired of playing with; their lives seemed to me a fate worse than death. And then one of those discarded puppets saw me and grinned and it was my father.

So when he died I was relieved. I would have helped him out. I had tried to 'kill' him, one way or another, many times before. As long as I can remember it seemed to me that I could not come fully alive until he was gone. At school I pretended to be an orphan; as a teenager I invented heroic deaths for him. After he told me the point at which he would want to die I often dreamed I was killing him.

But when the time came he didn't ask me. Our relationship had changed. The father in the man had died ten years ago, when we both stared at the tear-blurred outline of a bright green coral snake. He knew it too. His last message, the night he died, was to tell my mother not to let 'the girls' see his body. He wanted us to remember him as he used to be.

What remained were the questions. The death of a parent is one of the great universal experiences that shape our lives. It is supposed to be the final rite of passage to maturity, yet what persists are more questions than answers. There is an assumption, psychological and philosophical, that by answering questions with more questions we may arrive at a resolution. Perhaps that is the purpose of this book. We all face the death of our parents in imagination, but we can't practise for the reality. We can, perhaps, learn from others' experience to help us face the questions when it happens. So many questions. What is the nature of the relationship between parent and child? How are the deaths of mothers and fathers different? Who are our parents, anyway, when they are not mothers and fathers? Of all the men I have been close to, for instance, I now realise I did not know my father as a man at all. And do all children, like my sister and myself, know our common father completely differently? Do we invent our parents in our own image, as we feel our parents tried to invent us? What, indeed, *makes* a parent into a parent? And, above all, is the death of a parent really the end of the relationship?

These are the sorts of themes and dilemmas addressed by the writers who have contributed to this book. They all write out of their own experience of a parent's death. This is not a practical guide on how to handle death; it is a full-hearted invitation to the sharing of mind and spirit with men and women who have the power to capture their most intense feelings in words. Whatever the circumstances of a parent's death, there is a common bond in the experience. Cathartic is an overworked word, but I believe no one who has lost a parent can read these essays and not be moved and uplifted. Those seeking answers will achieve some kind of resolution.

For this, all the contributors have my grateful thanks, and my admiration. I am overwhelmed at the generosity with which they have shared deeply personal thoughts and feelings expressly for this collection. It is not easy. Novelists may explore their own feelings obliquely through their fictional characters, but they are deliberately not autobiographers. It is hard, too, for journalists to reveal themselves; they are used to projecting other people's emotions. Here both have responded to the subject of this book by transcending any inhibitions of form. To every one of them my thanks for undertaking an often painful task, and for what their achievement offers all of us who have ever lost, who must some time lose, a parent.

Jane McLoughlin

NINA BAWDEN

The Price of Living

My father died quite unexpectedly one Sunday lunchtime with his second pink gin in his hand. He was in his ninetieth year. A good exit, he would have said – indeed, often *had* said, commending some old friend or other for not 'hanging about' or 'being a burden'. Death was the price you paid for living. What he feared was the process of dying.

I loved my mother – and was a little afraid of her. She was iron-willed and competent in ways that I was not. After she died, my son, Robert, said he would always remember his grandmother's useful, determined hands; making pastry, fastening knots in shoelaces, unscrewing jam-jar lids – to the end of her life she had stronger wrists than any other woman I have known.

And, or so it seemed to me, she was without fear. I was afraid of spiders, of big, barking dogs, of the milkman's horse with its white, rolling eye. My mother fed the fat spider that lived above the kitchen sink, tossing dead flies into its dusty web, and she patted the horse on its pale, velvet nose. She tried to persuade me to offer it half an apple on my open palm, but I was too afraid of its teeth – so yellow and slimy and long.

That was when I was young. When I was older, I saw she was brave in other ways, too. My father was a marine engineer, at sea all my childhood. We lived in East London, near the docks. I had two younger brothers and my mother brought us up more or less on her own, with very little money. When the war came in 1939, although I was evacuated with the older of my two brothers, she stayed behind with Robin, the baby, and taught at a local school all through the London Blitz until Robin caught diphtheria and nearly died.

She spent the rest of the war in a farmhouse in Shropshire where I think she was happier than any other time in her adult life, but when the war ended, and my father retired, she came back to London without complaint. They moved to Kent and she started teaching again, in her fifties, so that there could be enough money to send Robin to a public school. She remained, in all our eyes, absolutely strong and dependable. One winter, she caught pneumonia and was taken into the cottage hospital; I went to see her and was unreasonably shocked to find her in bed. Oh, she was sitting up, smiling, but sitting up and smiling *in bed!* She said, 'Don't look so shocked, silly girl. I'll be out of here tomorrow.'

My father was twelve years older than she was. He died in 1976, the same year as her much loved older sister who had lived next door, and Robin and I persuaded her to move into London. She was seventy-eight then, still physically strong enough to walk several miles and jump on and off buses, and lively minded enough to make new friends, a new life for herself. She was about eighty-four when she began, very slowly, to be more dependent. She lived two doors away from my brother and his family and a mile away from me. Since I was the only adult able to organise my working life to suit myself, I visited her regularly; three or four times a week to begin with, once a day later on. She had a miniature schnauzer bitch she was devoted to. My brother, or my niece, walked Trinket in the mornings, I exercised her in the afternoons. Then my mother would make tea for me and a slice of toast that was always buttered to the *very edge*. She said, quite rightly, that it was the only way to butter toast. She began to repeat this rather frequently, several times every afternoon. When tea was over, I would fetch the sweet sherry from the corner cupboard and her best glasses, and we would watch *Nationwide* together.

Her other sister died, and my son, Niki, thirty-three and her oldest grandson. And one of her best friends from her teacher-training college. The last of her generation, she said, no one left. But the next day, when I thought she might want to talk about this friend, she had forgotten her name. She said that sometimes things slipped away. She said that she hoped her memory would 'see her out'. She said she hoped she might see her other son, Peter, who lived in Australia, once more before she died.

One day she was very aggrieved. She had jumped off a moving bus with Trinket in her arms. A man had caught her and said, 'You're too old to do that sort of thing at your age, m'darling.' From that day she began to walk like an old woman; chin thrust forward, bent over.

She took Trinket to the vet and had her destroyed. She said it was the only kind thing to do, since she would soon be unable to do anything for her. Afterwards – the next day – she said she thought she must have been mad.

Or prescient. (She had other 'powers', after all; she was a water diviner, and once, standing on the clifftop in Herne Bay, she said she was sure there had been an earthquake somewhere; we heard, on the six o'clock news, that there had been an earthquake in Turkey.) She was taken ill the next day, acute vomiting and diarrhoea, and in the hospital the surgeon diagnosed a twisted bowel. He said he was sorry, but he would have to operate. We didn't understand why he should feel the need to apologise, and he didn't explain. Didn't have time to, perhaps, because at that moment my mother, lying on the trolley, on her way to the operating theatre, launched into a dramatic and comprehensive deathbed farewell – to my brother and his wife, my husband and me. She had had a wonderful life; she didn't mind dying; we were to tell Peter, in Australia, that she would have waited for him to come if she had been able to; she sent her love to her grandchildren; her love to us all. By the time she had finished, even the surgeon was in tears. (Of course, he knew, as we did not, what the result of the anaesthetic could be.)

When she came round, she didn't know where she was. She knew the four of us, but not our children's names. The young surgeon came and sat beside her on the bed and held her hand and asked her how she felt and said he was delighted that the operation had been such a success. She seized her handbag with her free hand and hit him round the head with it. She said, 'Do you call it a success, young man, to drive an old woman out of her wits?'

Even then, we didn't understand. We told ourselves she was still a bit confused by the anaesthetic; she would be 'herself' in a day or two. A more urgent problem was where she was to go when she left hospital. Her own flat was out of the question; the Sister said she needed day and night nursing. I lived on five floors and had no suitable room – that is, no room with an adjacent bathroom. My brother and his wife were both out all day. Anyway, my mother had often said she didn't want to live with either of us; our houses were too inconvenient and too cold.

I was told to see the social worker. She was two hours late for our appointment; when she came she said no one had told her that I was waiting; she hadn't come earlier because most people didn't turn up on time. She was a pleasant girl, apparently eager to be helpful. She had a list of convalescent homes of which one was typical: a Salvation Army hostel on the south coast where patients had to make their own beds and be fit to climb stairs because there was no lift. I said that I didn't think that would be very suitable for a woman in her eighties who had just had a major abdominal operation. The young woman seemed surprised. I asked her if she had seen my mother and she shook her head. 'We like to see the families first,' she said.

It was quite a cunning move by the NHS, I thought. Offer only farcical possibilities and any family that is not totally destitute will make their own arrangement. Although when we did so, it turned out not much better. We drove my poor, bewildered mother to a highly recommended private nursing home in Wimbledon. They showed us into a room about ten foot by eight which contained two other aged persons. I said, 'My mother has never shared a room with a stranger in her life. I don't think this is a good time to begin.'

The nurse – a Sister, or a Matron? – smiled. 'You'll learn,' the smile said. She showed us into a narrow single room which was dull but adequate and we waited outside while my mother was helped into bed. When we came into the room she looked at us, terrified and angry, and began to cry. Her distress focused on a dreadful coloured picture on the wall – a picture of a leering and hideous clown. The nurse said, 'Most old people like that picture because it's nice and bright', and I decided that she must be deranged. Or drunk. A kind of Mrs Gamp. What were we doing? Were *we* drunk, or mad?

We took the picture off the wall and put it in the gimcrack wardrobe. My brother and I were as bewildered as my mother by the sudden and unexpected change in her; the headlong decline from powerful adult to shaken and frightened child. My brother wanted to take her home with him immediately. I hesitated. Mrs Gamp, all at once seeming much more kind and sensible, pointed out that my mother was exhausted by the journey and that she needed careful nursing which she hadn't had in hospital. 'You should see the wound,' she said, and clicked her tongue. 'I would never have sent a patient home in that condition from any ward of mine when I was Sister.'

Not only kind and sensible, I decided gratefully, but infinitely more capable than we were. Just a few days here and my mother would be physically stronger, better able to be moved to somewhere more suitable. We lived in Islington, a long way from Wimbledon. Why had we come here?

'Why on earth did we go there?' my brother asked as we drove home. 'It was what we could afford,' I said. 'Well,' he said, 'she can't stay there.' Guilt made us out of temper with each other.

After five days, Robin took her home with him. He had enough room; a wife and three growing children who were fond of her; a mother-in-law who was a saint. I would go in for part of every day, and we would employ what other help seemed needed. My mother was pleased to be there to begin with. But she grew increasingly suspicious; whenever anyone went out of the room she thought they were plotting against her. We thought it was no more than the loss of memory which we still innocently believed would repair itself with love and care and familiar people round her.

We asked if she felt well enough to go back to her flat; there was a woman who had helped her in the house who was willing to move in and look after her. My mother became very agitated. She announced that she wished to go into a home, 'where she could be looked after properly'. This was a decision entirely in character – in spite of her increasing dementia, her personality seemed quite unchanged. She had always had a kind of impatient courage that not only met life head on, but made her go forward to meet it. If a home and professional care was inevitable, better sooner rather than later. 'If it's got to be, it's best to get it over with,' she said. 'I'd like to get it off my mind.'

We looked at a number of what seemed to us terrible places. There was a home on the fringes of London where the inmates (known as 'guests') were watched through a television monitor. And at another, the nurse who was showing us round suddenly flung open a door, gestured at an old man lying in bed, his bony nose pointing at the ceiling, and said, with a bright, conspiratorial leer, 'You can see this room's likely to be vacant by the end of the week.' Eventually we settled on a half-private, half-charitable institution in north London, beguiled by a pretty, youngish, rather gushing Matron, fresh flowers in the hall, and a smell of polish instead of disinfectant.

We took my mother there. She said, accusingly, when we were being shown around the garden, 'Where are all the happy old ladies laughing and talking under the chestnut tree?', and we knew that we had failed her. Leaving her there was like abandoning a child to strangers. A hurt and angry child. And, as if she were speaking about a child, the pretty Matron said, 'Don't worry, she'll settle down once you've gone. But don't come too often for the first week or two, let her get used to us.'

This home did not, as a policy, admit people with senile dementia. My mother had a sense of propriety and a good social manner which had concealed her true condition from us, from the Matron, and even, for a while, from the sympathetic doctor who had examined her. But her co-prisoners were sharper. Scenting in my mother the weakness that they feared lay in wait for them around the next corner, they turned on her like savage children. They hid her handbag. They whispered between themselves when she came into a room and they laughed at her when she turned her back to leave. Driven to despair she telephoned the four of us in turn, sometimes weeping, sometimes raving like a lunatic. She wrote scrawling, frantic, accusing letters. Were we quite heartless? She had taken care of us, had we no thought for her, no room in our lives, no chimney corner? It was painful beyond words – and frightening.

She refused to eat. I found jam sandwiches hidden in her shoes. She said they were trying to poison her. Then she had a fall and was taken to hospital. The X-ray showed nothing wrong. But she was crying with pain; insisting she couldn't stand up, couldn't get off the bed. The Matron said, 'She is trying to get attention. She is a manipulative woman, your mother.'

I said, 'She's in pain. Anyone can see she's in pain.'

The home doctor called a geriatric psychiatrist to visit her; a careful, concerned woman who comforted us all. She admitted my mother to an acute psychiatric unit: a pleasant, old-fashioned, rambling building near Highgate Woods. She was X-rayed again, more carefully, and found to have a crush fracture of the spine which must, the psychiatrist said, have been agonising. They treated the injury, coaxed her to walk again and, with what seemed to us miraculous skill, managed to calm her damaged mind. They played card games and word games with her, and were delighted when she won at Scrabble.

When they had time, they took her to the woods in a wheelchair; they washed her hair and did her nails, treating her always with respect and with dignity. It became a pleasure to visit her. I took Niki's daughter to see her and she was a smiling great-grandmother, a bit forgetful, but asking the right questions about school, boyfriends and going to university.

They couldn't keep her for ever. This was an acute unit; she had already stayed longer than the rules allowed. After three months we must find somewhere else for her. But the unit would help us to make the decision; she would spend a day in each place we suggested, and a nurse would go and spend the day with her and see how she reacted. 'She might have a little trouble remembering how she really felt otherwise,' they said tactfully.

The nurse was a tall young man my mother was especially fond of. He insisted that she appeared not only to understand the choice she was making but also that it was Hobson's Choice; nowhere could be perfect. They settled on a large home run by Islington Council that had an exceptionally sensitive and energetic Matron, small but decent rooms and – something that seemed to me important – an always open office where the residents could wander in at will to talk to the Matron, or to get lights for their cigarettes, stamps for their letters.

Although my mother wept when she left the unit, kissing the nurses and thanking them, saying, 'My dears, I have been so happy here,' she was not *unhappy* in her new home. Or, rather, when she was unhappy, she never told Robin or me. She once said to my husband, who was taking her along the corridor to her room after a day spent with us, 'Oh, Austen, I don't like it here, but you mustn't tell Nina.' But the rage and despair she had felt to begin with seemed to fade as her memory faded; as her grasp on reality loosened.

I was sitting with her in her little room one winter afternoon. She said, 'What's outside this room, Nina? I know I ought to know, but I can't remember.' I described the long, bare corridor that she didn't much care for, the lift at the end, the dining room that would be laid now for supper, the large living room with the television and the awful plastic daffodils. She nodded. She said, 'I believe you. But it seems to me that we are sitting here alone, in a small, bright capsule, spinning through the dark.' And she said to Austen, when he picked her up on Easter Sunday, 'It seems dreadful, but I have forgotten what Easter is *for*. Though I know it is something important.'

She never forgot us. And she remembered the children's names now. She knew Niki was dead, and spoke of him lovingly. She knew that Robert was a doctor and that Perdita was in the theatre and that my brother's children were all still at school. But when Perdita had a baby and we took my mother to the hospital, she cuddled the tiny, swaddled girl – who had been brought out of an incubator to meet her great-grandmother – and said, 'Is it *mine?*' We reassured her and she seemed relieved. She said, 'How clever of you, Perdita.' We beamed; we thought Perdita was clever, too. But this was not what my mother meant. The maternity ward at St Bartholomew's Hospital was full of visiting fathers. Husbands. My mother looked at them with contempt and said, very loudly and clearly, 'So clever to get a baby without having to put up with one of *those*.'

We went away for three months. It had been planned long ago. I telephoned from abroad and was told she was well. Coming back, I was nervous. How could I have left her so long? But when we walked in, Austen and I, she looked at us smiling. 'How lovely to see you, how good of you to come again so soon, you were only here yesterday.'

But she was helpless. That is the thing I remember. This strong, brave woman who had been used all her life to running her own affairs, making decisions for herself and for others, was at the mercy of people who might be kind most of the time but could be insensitive, lazy, forgetful. She was deaf; she was always losing her hearing aid. Or it needed a battery. She couldn't read the newspaper or a letter. It was a while before we found out that she had been given new glasses but they were only for distance. She had never worn distance glasses and didn't understand why she couldn't read with them. And there was the tyranny of enforced entertainment. And worse! One Friday I found the big living room invaded by a strident horde of hellfire alarmists from the local Baptist church; a preacher waving his arms about, threatening the innocent souls in his captive audience with eternal damnation, and a pianist thumping out the accompaniment to noisy hymns of a violent nature.

My mother was looking bemused. I took her away, and we sat outside the entrance, on the bench where the old men went to smoke, cigarette stubs round our feet. I thought of complaining to Islington Council, a leftish regime that would be hard pressed to make the proper reaction. They would naturally be against thrusting religion down the throats of these defenceless, elderly people. But then, consider! These Baptists were black. It might be racist to object to them . . .

They came out of the home at the same moment that a group of Hasidim passed by; men with skull-caps and beards, little, dark boys with long ringlets, on their way to synagogue. We watched as the two groups met on the pavement. They didn't look at each other, not one glance, but they parted smoothly, each allowing the other to pass through their midst without hindrance. 'Like the Red Sea,' my mother said, and laughed.

She had trouble breathing one night. The night staff called an ambulance. They telephoned us and we went to the hospital. We found the casualty department in uproar. I think it was a Saturday night. No one seemed to have heard of my mother. At last we found her behind a flowered curtain, trying to get off a trolley: a young woman doctor wrestling with her, trying to make her lie down, and all the time shouting at her. She said, to us, 'How can I take a history from this old woman if she refuses to tell me what's wrong with her?' She was blazing with fury – exhaustion too, probably, but in the circumstances that did not seem much mitigation. We pointed out that my mother was senile. I said, 'It happened here, in this hospital, it was the anaesthetic.' She turned her anger – and her weary frustration – on me. 'Do you mean you are *blaming the hospital?*' My mother said, 'Oh, Nina, I'm glad you've come, would you explain to this poor young woman that I'm not trying to escape, that I just want to go to the lavatory?'

She died in another hospital. She had pneumonia. It was a terminal ward, glittery with Christmas decorations. We went to see her on Christmas morning. We were not the first visitors. The mayor and his male companion had been to the ward, taken presents, given each patient a card, signed by both of them. Their relationship, the Sister said, had puzzled some of the older ladies. We gave my mother a necklace of ceramic beads and she held it to her face, trying to look at it. Her hands moved very slowly and her eyes looked different; greener than usual, and shining, but somehow unseeing. Her face had colour, but the flesh seemed to have shrunk away from her cheekbones since we had seen her the evening before. I said, 'I wish you were having Christmas dinner with us, Mum, instead of in this mouldy old hospital,' and found myself choking on tears. She said, sounding quite strong and cheerful, 'I shall enjoy thinking about you all but I'm more comfortable here.'

They telephoned from the hospital while Robin was carrying in the flaming Christmas pudding. When we got to the ward, the doctor and the staff nurse had whisky and tea waiting for us. One of them told me that she had been sitting beside her bed, with her Christmas glass of wine, when she suddenly shouted, 'I'm finished!' She had always had a good sense of theatre.

A tumour in her lung had burst. It was a mercy; they would have had to put her through painful tests to discover the nature of the cancer that killed her. I said, angrily, 'But she never smoked in her life,' and the doctor said, gently, 'She was old, dear, it sometimes happens when people are old.' It is often very soothing, the comfort of strangers.

We drank our tea and whisky and went home. We drew the curtains to darken the room; Robin lit the pudding again and we ate it with brandy butter. We pulled the crackers with the children. I thought – well, this is what it is like. Pieces of yourself fall away. When my son had died, when the police found him in the river, it had been a visceral pain: a disembowelment. This, my mother's death, was different; more like losing part of one's life rather than part of one's body; a link broken with the past, with a long-ago childhood. I remember my babies when they were born, exactly how they looked, each of them, the first time I saw them. No one now to remember me; no one to call me a 'silly girl', or to say, 'Trust you, Nina!' or, 'Nina, you *would*!'

I said, incompetently helping to clear up in the kitchen, 'Robin, d'you know what? We are orphans now.'

There were odds and ends of her life to be tidied away. I took a black bin bag of old clothes from the home and the hospital, and found the pathos of the things she had left behind almost unbearable. There was a watch we had bought her with a big, clear face, Roman numerals, but it was broken. There were some pieces of jewellery. The furniture from her flat, crockery, books, none of these things had the throat-catching impact of something she had worn, a blouse she had been fond of, a pair of shabby slippers . . .

I had been about ten. I had come home from school and her shoes were steaming in front of the fire. She was wearing slippers. She said, 'I got caught in the rain,' and turned the shoes over to get the heat to the soles. There were holes the size of a penny. I said, 'You ought to get your shoes mended,' and she laughed. She said, 'They're the only shoes I've got, silly girl.'

I remembered how little she took for herself. My father was away at sea; she hardly ever went out. My father was anxious about money. My mother may have been; if she was she never showed it. It wasn't until after my father retired, that she had a holiday; they went to Ireland with friends, to New Guinea to see their son, Peter.

Guilt flooded in, self-indulgent, as guilt always is. There was the day she had telephoned me to say there were white horses and a band on Highbury Fields, a celebration for May Day, and I had said, no, I couldn't come now, I wanted to finish writing my chapter. And another time, further back, just before my daughter was born when she had travelled from Kent to look after the boys and help with the new baby. She came, looking cold and tired; she had had a long, chilly train journey, from Kent, across London, to Surrey. I was doing the ironing and didn't stop until it was finished, not even to kiss her, make her a cup of tea. And, of course, above all, I should never have left her to die alone in the hospital.

There were almost certainly other occasions, but these are the ones I remember.

I was at a loss in the afternoons now, without occupation. Once, between three o'clock and six, I had thought I had too much to do. I had wrenched myself away from my computer, from my oh-so-important 'work', to walk my mother's stupid, elderly dog, be given tea and toast, drink sweet sherry (which I didn't much care for) while we watched *Nationwide*. Now those hours stretched out, grey and listless with boredom. There seemed no way of filling them. Unless someone came to see me, I lay on my bed in a kind of stupor, trying to go to sleep, to make the time pass until Austen came home. Or we went out to dinner. I had felt like this after Niki had died four years earlier; the late afternoon was his lowest point of the day and we would go for a walk, or go to the cinema. I had got through that, I told myself; this should be easier. A parent's death is part of life; a natural progression. Leaving their children on the last barricade. Among the grown-ups at last.

I did other things in the late afternoons. Now, only a distant sadness touches me sometimes; around five o'clock in the summer, earlier in the winter, when it begins to get dark. I think, I should have looked after them better. Both my son and my mother. I know better now about old age, the falling away, the senility. But there are no second chances.

Sometimes I catch myself in the mirror, looking a bit like my mother. Pursing my mouth as she did when she was concentrating on something. Talking to myself the way she did occasionally, when she thought she was alone. A fussy little whisper, or mutter. I used to think she was making plans, plotting; now I think she may have been talking to someone she didn't see any longer but suspected might be lurking somewhere quite close, around the next corner.

LUCY ELLMANN

Penance Soup

A day is like two weeks to a bird. Buttercups really are cups. I divulge these titbits as a natural attempt to evade thinking about my parents' deaths. For there's nothing natural about parents dying. There's nothing natural about death at all. Nothing *else* in the world is eternal! It's an aberration, a cosmic mistake. It shouldn't be allowed. How can love and death *both* be natural? They belong on separate planets.

Death has no relevance for me, I don't need it. I lead an undramatic sort of existence, and am never *nice* enough to anybody. Death just doesn't fit into my scheme of things. It's very out of fashion. It only happens to the careless, the obese, smokers, joggers and people who place themselves in the hands of the Wrong Doctor. And even though my relatives have a tendency to smoke, eat too much and choose the Wrong Doctor, it doesn't strike me as comfortingly 'natural' to shove the people who brought me up into the ground.

So here I am, an oversized orphan. Too old to be Heidi, too fat to get adopted. I used to think being an orphan would be romantic. As a child, I perfected sad expressions and trudged through the streets, hoping people would think I was all alone in the world. Now I *am* all alone in the world and it's not romantic. It's sort of dingy and monotonous. It's an eternal bedtime, it's feeding cats, watering flower bulbs that don't sprout, it's shyness, Kleenexes and coal buckets, defencelessness and hoping to be rescued, a world without reward. It's penance soup, full of Pooh-sticks, pebbles and slime.

My grief lacks charm of any kind. It sometimes takes the form of eating spaghetti, in the *morning*. I neglect myself to emphasise the fact that no one cares any more if I neglect myself. I'm old before my time, and living proof that not every experience enriches you as a human being. I haven't grown in any way (except in width). I'm less than I was: less compassionate, less tolerant, less generous, less capable of love. I have a horror of illness, in myself and others. Likewise, old age. I have sympathy only for people who seem to resemble my parents, and I avoid these if possible. I have little interest in anyone, especially if they appear to be needy, this aversion often degenerating into deep antipathy. Any prejudices I ever had are now worse, my thinking screwier, and all other incapacities continually on the increase. I trudge, truly sad now, under the weight of lethargy, laxity and a lack of libido. Most of the time I'm no use to anybody. The rest of the time I function but it feels fake.

At the height of my inability to function, I somehow managed to acquire a bereavement counsellor. The study of bereavement is clearly in its infancy. My bereavement counsellor coped with my parents' deaths little better than I. She placed her trust in a few theories and a plan of action she'd picked up somewhere. Her plan: to work through the three stages of bereavement in six one-hour sessions. Thus, two hours for denial, two for guilt, two for anger, I guess. I should have known I wasn't up to the rigours of this regime. I've always been easily fatigued, and the pace of this was somewhat ambitious. My father died seven years ago, my mother five, and I'm barely through 'denial' *now*!

Another stricture was that I was not supposed to turn up to our meetings depressed, since this inhibited our progress. Unfortunately, I was rather attached to my depression at the time and found it hard to leave it at home. But the worst request my counsellor came up with was that I should eliminate one parent from the discussion – she could only 'work' on one bereavement at a time! How was I to know which bereavement was afflicting me more, which bereavement made me want to stay in bed all day, which particular bereavement made me catatonic, which splendid bereavement I should cleave to most passionately? This was 'Sophie's Choice', in reverse. I chose my mother and still feel guilty about it.

It suggests to me that the Bereavement Brigade can't face death either, just like the rest of us. They want it packaged and frozen before they'll touch it. The red raw stuff is simply not manageable, not bearable. There's nowhere for it to be safely emitted. It's radioactive and it lasts for ever.

This is where the stiff upper lip comes into its own. Americans go all soft and floppy about death. They're shocked and horrified and resort without warning to mysticism or sentimentality. The British instead go silent and concentrate on practicalities – it's a mercy to anyone in the vicinity. And it's brave. This is how they survived the Blitz. Americans would have gone to pieces.

I'm American enough to go to pieces and British enough to find this failure annoying. Which is why I cling to the fact that a day is like two weeks to a bird, and buttercups really are cups.

GILLIAN SLOVO

A Soft Target

The man behind the counter had a beard. He looked at my passport and then at me. He said, 'Ring your sister Robyn or Susie. Do you understand?'

I understood perfectly. I had lived my life in the expectation that death would suddenly hit out: now the only real unknown was at who.

I had spent a sleepless night on a ferry from Spain but was no longer tired. Without speaking I sat as Andy steered the car through Customs. We drove to the nearest phone box.

Many years ago, in South Africa, my sister Shawn and I had waited by the phone as hailstones shrouded the lawn. Our grandmother had gone to visit our mother in prison and hadn't returned. And so we sat, waiting for the call which would tell us that, after the disappearances of father, mother and grandfather, something had happened to this, our last remaining adult.

That time the panic was wasted. Our grandmother appeared, complaining about the traffic. And so that little voice – the one that said I should always be on guard, that I should never go anywhere, especially not on a touring camping holiday – was temporarily quelled.

The car was parked on the wrong side of the road. I crossed over, thinking it must be my father who'd died. Since being made chief of staff of the ANC's army, Umkhonto we Sizwe, he was the one with the protective AK47 in the wardrobe – my mother's weapons were less tangible, the words she used as she wrote and taught and the fierceness of her intellect.

A red phone box in Portsmouth. What am I doing here? I thought as my fingers tapped out numbers. Robyn was engaged. I phoned Susie. She told me – it was my mother. My mother whom I'd last seen the day before she had left to go back to Mozambique, the day before I'd gone on holiday. She'd been killed, in Maputo where she lived, in the university where she worked, by a parcel bomb that they had sent to her.

I phoned my grandmother. Who said, 'They killed her, Gilly' – she's the only person who called me this '– and you weren't here.'

When last I'd seen her, my mother had talked of how she had told my grandmother, her mother, to stop complaining and reach out for what she wanted. 'Life's too short' were the words she had used; 'you never know what will happen.' I'd witnessed her pleasure: she had done something, at last, to short-circuit the undercurrent of guilt that ran between her and her mother. But she had been talking of her eighty-year-old mother's imminent death – not of her own.

When I arrived in Mozambique my father told me that on the morning before she had been killed he had awakened early and looked at her and thought: she looks dead.

There it was again – that anticipation of death which was supposed to protect us from shock. Was it us, only, who experience it?

Perhaps not. Since my mother's death, someone else told me the same story – how she had awakened a few mornings before her partner's sudden death and had a presentiment of what was to come.

We drove to Heathrow. Two thoughts recurred. The first strangely reassuring – that just because I had always feared this would happen, this did not mean I was madly neurotic. The other thought – that I would have a child – was more uncomfortable. I pushed it away, got on with the business of checking in.

It was my day for beards – the man who escorted us to the plane had one too.

I wasn't scared of flying – not this time. My plane phobia had been about leaving places, about travelling into the unknown, about what would happen while I was out of touch. Nothing to fear now – it had already happened.

We landed in Zimbabwe. We had eight hours to wait before we could get to Mozambique. We checked in at a hotel, took a shower, dressed in the borrowed clothes that friends had brought to the airport. I thought about the fact that I had not said a proper goodbye to my mother, that in my last glimpse of her face I had seen hurt from the tensions unsaid between us.

Her best friend told me later that my mother had understood. 'Understood what?' I asked. 'That you needed to be left on your own,' she said. I shook my head but it was too late to tell my mother that what I had really wanted was something much more intangible. Her recognition, perhaps – or was it reparation? – for the strain that her life had imposed on me.

I no longer need that from her. In the eleven years since she died, I have had to face our entanglement on my own. But then I ask myself: if she had lived would I have continued to be trapped in a struggle to get from her what was mine to find?

My father was at the foot of the stairs. We hugged. I felt his arms, dammed up by what he had to endure. A man from protocol took our passports and showed us to the car. We drove. Through road blocks . . . to a concert hall. Abdullah Ibrahim had been in the country and, hearing of Ruth's death, had put on a special concert for her. So I was seated behind a row of government ministers, beside the family that I hadn't yet had time to even greet, my feelings battling with the exigencies of a public scrutiny, listening to the sweet sorrow of one exile to another.

There was a photograph of Ruth on stage. Ruth as she had been in the last year of her life – her hair fuzzing out in the way it would always have done if not for the legions of hairdressers that trained it into line. She was smiling, in that photograph, the contented person she had become in Mozambique.

Mozambique was the home she found for herself. After years of struggling to feel part of English life, southern Africa had reclaimed her. And it changed her. Her face relaxed, she laughed more often. She was finally part of a society of which she could approve and part of a movement where what she had to offer was valued.

But was there more than that? Was it the fact that this was a country she came to, originally on her own? To work in Mozambique she left her mother and her daughters behind – and left behind also the guilt that her activism and her work had always provoked. In other families, the children cut loose: in mine it was the parents.

Mozambique had changed her in countless ways. I remember how, on a visit to London, she, normally so decisive, dithered in front of a delicatessen counter. Coming from a country where there was either one, or (and this was the normal state of affairs) no cheese, the sheer range of what was displayed in front of her bewildered her. In the end she asked me to choose.

But perhaps this unexpected indecision signalled a deeper change in her. Perhaps, having finally left home, she could turn to me, her daughter, for advice, however trivial.

Increasingly I'm told I look like her. 'It's like sitting behind a ghost,' someone said the other day. I never was like her before – this is my years advancing. I have reached the age she was when we arrived in England, the age at which many here met her and therefore the age at which they remember her.

I am changing. She stays the same, that picture of her on my wall, smiling with the light glimmering in her hair. Slowly I catch up with her, edging towards the time when she, so alive, was killed.

The concert ended and we were taken to the home I'd not

previously seen. The last time I'd been to visit them, my parents had lived elsewhere, in the south of the city, in a flat overlooking the estuary. I remembered waking to the sounds of her dawn typing.

That time my mother had found difficulty letting go of me. She'd encouraged Andy and I to travel, had cut through reams of red tape to get us the correct permission. We'd gone by bus to Xai-Xai, the only pleasure-seekers in the country, and stayed in a hotel big enough to house the hordes of South African tourists that no longer came. She let us go, but at the last minute she panicked, rushed to the bus station, not entirely sure that Andy and I were grown up enough to do it on our own.

The morning after her death, I woke early. Not from her typing but from the lack of it. I walked with my father by the seaside. We didn't talk. As the day began we drove to the hospital, to see Bridget who had been caught up in the blast. Her eardrum had burst, her eyes had been affected, and because of this she was under strict instructions from the doctor not to cry. We talked, both of us trying to keep our eyes dry.

We didn't have to organise the funeral.

I have endured the death of one of my mother's best friends since then, have watched her children planning each moment of their saying goodbye to make it exactly what they wanted. It was not like that for us. Everything – the speakers, the transport, the singing – was done by others, many of them strangers to me.

We sat in her house until the time was ready. While ANC women kept on cooking, the doorbell rang as others came to visit. We, her mother, Joe and her three daughters, living under the same roof for the first time in years. The fierce bonds that had always tied us, her girls together, and the competitiveness for family attention that had always been there, our constant companion. And she was not there to arbitrate.

The day came. We were put in large black cars, driven to each venue. The first, a kind of non-religious chapel. Outside, a crowd of people singing; inside, the dark interior. A group of dignitaries waited beside the coffin. It was closed – on my father's request.

I was grateful then that I did not have to see her in front of those embarrassed, uncomfortable men. And yet would it have helped to see what she looked like after she died?

There is nothing in my imagination that can tell me. When I think of it, I see what my father saw after they called him in – her legs and, untouched at their end, a pair of elegant, undamaged high-heeled shoes that were her passion. He, who had witnessed death by violence before, didn't go any further.

I would not have either. And yet, perhaps, if I had seen her, some part of my horror at what the explosion must have done to her might have been laid to rest.

When we walked out into the dazzling light, our car had disappeared. 'Run out of petrol', someone explained, a singularly Mozambiquan experience. We waited, shuffling, smoking cigarettes until somehow, somewhere they managed to find enough to go on.

The cemetery was an alien thing – a walled enclosure with little caskets cut out of stone, each holding another person's ashes. Ruth was to be buried amongst the other South Africans who had been killed in Mozambique. We stood in the dryness of the cracked, parched earth as speeches jolted over us. This was the mother I didn't want to mourn – this heroine of an epic struggle.

I remembered her talking at the memorial for her friend Hilary. She spoke of the public Hilary and of the private one as well – of Hilary's flamboyant self, expressed in her love of huge hats.

So many funerals.

I remember her telling me how, at another funeral, she had spoken of the woman who had died, contrasting her to the men in double-breasted suits – the champions of the Soviet communism she despised.

But at my mother's funeral there was no reference to her wardrobe, she who had allowed herself to be taken to prison only after she'd packed silk underwear. Her death had made her public property. They spoke of her achievements, not of who she was.

The more they talked the less could I conjure her up. And yet I knew that she deserved no less. She had seemed so fearless in life: she had always risen to any challenge, but she had also been driven by self-doubt and by the sense of her own inadequacy. This large crowd that gathered by her graveside was what she deserved – but it was not something that she might have expected.

She came back to me afterwards, the person she had been to me. I remember her as I had said goodbye that one last time – her smile which contained within it awkwardness. I remember other occasions – her working, with the same passion she reserved for everything, on a jigsaw puzzle. Her manic playing of the game of patience I had recently taught her. Her speaking to me of our relationship in a Maputo ice-cream parlour that hadn't stocked ice-cream for the past six months. It was those occasions, the ones I could conjure up at will, that I thought I would never forget.

But as time progresses, each year counted as one more since she died, my memories begin to lapse.

There are concrete ways of registering the changes. When my sister Shawn was writing *A World Apart* we talked of the past and of who Ruth had been. I was so clear then about the line that divided the reality from the fiction. And when before the film was made I met Barbara Hershey, the actress who was to play Ruth, I thought: she is nothing like my mother.

I am no longer so sure. Without our mother there to arbitrate, we sometimes have disagreements as to which parts of the film were real and which were fiction. And on the tube the other day, I saw a poster advertising a Barbara Hershey film and for a moment, I thought: 'There's my mother.'

If I had been asked what I wanted for her dead body, I would have chosen cremation. And yet the burial, as lines of mourners threw spadefuls of brown earth on to her coffin until it was covered, was, for me, the essence of her funeral. I need only to look at the television, to see those countless other burials, that same singing, that same spirit of defiance, to remember how hers had been. At the time I noticed other things as well – the young boy who pushed himself into line, shovelling dirt with vigour, her funeral a backdrop to his fantasy about heroism and the struggle.

When it was over she lay there – one white woman amongst thirteen black men all killed by the same enemy. And then we left.

She lay there and we kept on moving.

My life has changed since then. I see her death as a watershed, a reference back to what has been transformed. I was childless when she died – yesterday my daughter turned eight. I had never had a book published – now I am a writer of fiction.

And it's not only my immediate world that changed. Everything else has also been put on its head – everything she held dear. Soon after she died, Samora Machel was forced to sign the Nkomati accord and the ANC was evicted from Mozambique. What would she have thought of this – she who saw the world through such clear eyes? Could she have forgiven the cynical realism that has replaced the utopianism of the country she adopted? And those other transformations – the end of a Soviet Union which she, a communist, had always considered so deficient. What would she have said of the vacuum that has slipped into its place?

More also. Eight years after her death, she could have gone to South Africa; ten years after they held a commemoration for her in Cape Town. That's a bigger puzzle – how she would have fitted there in that turbulent, wonderful, contradictory, vicious society that never before would give her a place, that had killed her and now begins to honour her.

That country where her murderers go free – could even, perhaps, be encountered, smiling at a cocktail party.

I did not want revenge, not for many years. I looked at people who had lost relatives violently and who cried out for blood and I didn't understand them. I told myself that it was easier for me, that my mother died violently but for a reason, a cause which gave meaning to her life and her death alike.

And then I watched others in South Africa shaking the hand of those who tortured them and I thought: how can they?

It makes me wonder whether my refusal to contemplate revenge was merely self-protection. I didn't want to think about her killers – to dwell on them would give them too much status. I'd never wanted to meet them – to see their faces. I had nothing to say to them – they would not be good enough for her.

But maybe it was more than that: maybe what I feared hearing was how they had done it routinely, unthinking, targeting her not because of who she was, but because she was just an enemy who could be reached. A soft target.

Before her death South Africa was a country which, even in thought I had avoided. It had caused me too much pain – it wasn't mine, it was hers. But as we sat, sitting our own special kind of shiva, an old man turned to me. 'Ruth has had to give up the spear,' he said. 'You must take it from her.'

Her reach was too long – her hold too certain – her spear was not mine to take. And yet her death meant I could no longer ignore South Africa. I used what happened in my fiction, to help me come to terms with it. I wrote *Ties of Blood* because I was trying to find my past. Her past.

Her death made of me an adult. It made me face what I had always hoped I might avoid, and it made me define myself not in opposition or competition to who she was but by myself.

And yet there is so much she didn't live to tell me.

Growing old, for example. She never did that. She was a woman proud of her appearance: she would not have liked the ravages of time.

But maybe, I tell myself, she had the capacity to accept them. Maybe she, who had found contentment in the storminess of Mozambique's transition, would have risen also to the challenge of growing old – not like her own mother who endured life, clinging grimly on until past ninety, until she forgot she ever had a daughter.

My daughter has Ruth as a middle name but Ruth is an abstract to her. Sometimes when I look at her I see my younger sister, Robyn, my mother's daughter whom my mother once abandoned to me – the fuel for many of our quarrels. It doesn't matter any longer. We've all grown since then – we who were adults at her death have grown up after it.

She was a hard act to follow. A powerful, clever, driven woman who cut a path for herself, alone, without a women's movement for help or company.

The cost she paid for what she did was arduous. But I paid it too. We used to argue about it – her way versus mine. I wanted more than she could give. I wanted her to be who she was, determined, active, unstinting, but I wanted her also to be all to me. Now I have a child and now I know that no woman could do what I asked of her.

I've grown and she has not. In the conversations I have with her, she never ages. Death stops – it is irrevocable – while we continue. Her public persona is perpetuated, more dominant than before. I have learned things about her, private things, that she did not tell me. I have seen her through the eyes of others, listened to their conflicting impressions, and without her there to adjudicate, I have had to see her for myself. She is frozen in all our memories: what my sisters have kept of her, is theirs alone. What I have, is mine.

I look to the brass tortoise that was hers – which she kept on her desk and I keep on mine – and I don't know whether, had she lived, I would have come to the same sense of peace I now feel for her. I wonder, even as I think of her, what we could have done together to release me, eventually, from behind her shadow. I will never know.

BRUCE KENT

Repeating the Pattern

My own parents died in the same place: St Joseph's Hospice in Hackney, where both had been private, long-term residents and patients.

My father died in 1972 and my mother in 1980, which reversed the order we had all expected. My mother in 1972 was clearly losing weight and going downhill fast. My father, whose problem was a kind of early senility, used to come down from his room on the male floor above to visit her. It was strange to see this man in a wheelchair, who had been so devoted and loving during their marriage, opening the door of her little locker, and methodically pinching her sweets while she lay, half in and half out of consciousness, on her bed at his side.

But what looked inevitable took another direction. He, one lunchtime, got some food lodged in his throat, developed bronchitis, and was at death's door by the evening. I was urgently called to the hospice. When I finally arrived I met a priest whom I did not know, and who did not know me, coming down the stairs. 'There is no need to go in,' said he, 'I've anointed Mr Kent and said the prayers for the dying.' Thus I learned that my father was on his way.

When I got to the bedside I witnessed a scene I shall never forget. My father was under some kind of plastic tent receiving oxygen. At each side of him there was a nun – two of the many who had given him such loving care during his months in the hospice. They were repeating 'Jesus, Mary, Joseph, help' over and over again while holding his hands and encouraging him to say the words himself. After a little while his struggle to breathe just came quietly to an end. A man, who once had little time for priests and nuns, died almost in their arms.

I went off that night in a kind of daze. To the best of my knowledge my mother was coming to the end of her time in the ward below. It was late at night but I had to tell my brother and sister. There were arrangements of all sorts to be made, though I could barely remember what they were. It was not a moment for tears. In a strange way I was somehow out of myself, almost watching the situation as if it was someone else's drama. The tears only came late that night when I had to send a telegram to our relations in Canada to tell them what had happened. I wrote out the message. 'Kenneth has died and Mollie is slipping away' was what I wanted to say.

But I couldn't. I just choked. The operator could not have been more kindly. Such messages must have been commonplace to him. 'Take your time,' he said. 'Let's go back to the beginning. What was the address?' Without his help I don't think I could have sent that telegram at all.

It was not actually an accurate message. No one knows why, but Mollie managed a U-turn. Physically she got much better and even put on weight. Her memory never recovered but her sense of humour and determination not to be beaten certainly did. I can still see her bright little blue eyes looking at me now, as ready to pull my leg as I was to pull hers. She recovered so well that she was even able to live with my sister for some years before she finally returned to St Joseph's and died eight years later. She loved being told that, at least in the competition not to get to the pearly gates first, she had beaten her Kenneth and had had the last word. That made up for a lot of the last words she did not get in while he was around.

In the June of 1980 her moment came too. By the time I got to the hospice she had already died and was being laid out, with a large brass crucifix between her hands on the white counterpane. Her funeral took place at the Catholic church at the bottom of Hoop Lane in Golders Green, where for years she had attended the Sunday morning eight o'clock Mass, and where so many family events had taken place: baptisms, marriages, and even my first Mass as a priest. Kenneth, eight years before, went to the crematorium only a few hundred yards away. Both her body and his ashes now lie, marked with a large simple reddish headstone, in the West Hampstead Cemetery. Once or twice a year I still go there to pull up a few weeds and wipe the stone clean of bird droppings and bits of mud.

All this is quite an ordinary story. These were not violent deaths, the result of war or unexpected accident. They were not untimely deaths, or deaths which divide families, as some families are divided over wills and property. Theirs were the ordinary deaths of good people, loved by their families and many others as well. They had both lived full lives up to and over the three score years and ten. We had all had plenty of time to prepare ourselves for what was coming.

My relationship with each of them was rather different. With my mother I had never had problems. The war had not separated us, we shared the same faith; and I had some of her open nature – which meant that she was never without friends. My relationship with my father had not always been easy. The war had separated him from his family, since we spent over three years in Canada as evacuees. I came back as a teenager to meet a man I did not know, who had a very powerful personality, who was kindly, but who could be embarrassingly over-generous. He also had the ability to be very verbally cruel when drunk. I did not know what being drunk meant until I realised one night that despite the help of the little wartime blackout torch he could not even get his key into the lock on our front door.

He was a man both to admire and to fear. As a teenager I would sometimes pray that I would not be left alone with him in the dining room while my mother went to get the next course from the kitchen. What to say? Do I risk a joke? Will he listen? I think he was also often at sea with a son he did not understand.

The family row that resulted when I wanted to go off to train for the priesthood was I suppose not unlike the rows that other families have over other issues. But I did not know about other people's family rows. Ours was an unequal relationship, which only began to level out when, in my father's judgement, I seemed to be on the ladder of success in the church career that I had chosen. He may not have known much about monsignors, but someone who had become the secretary to a cardinal must surely be following in the footsteps of the successful company managing director that he was.

The relationship became unequal in my favour when a kind of mixed depression and senility set in towards the last years of his life. Roles then reversed. I became the one who was immediately available, on whom he could lean. I took over the practicalities of repairs, rates, insurance, bank statements and the like. When he finally moved to St Joseph's I, living in London without family responsibilities, was able to be the regular visitor. Many times I drove him around London in an old converted ambulance which I bought for the purpose. It fitted his wheelchair excellently and he loved seeing his old haunts.

So death in his case, as in hers, was one point on a gradual process. Was that then the end of that? Close the books, enjoy happy memories, and put them in a few prayers once or twice a year?

It has not been like that. Despite the problems, few people can have had as secure a home as I had. It was always somewhere to come back to. There was always something in the fridge. Home was where I could bring my friends. In the army I would make impossible train journeys to be able to spend a few hours on leave with my family. If I needed money I had only to send a letter or a telegram. My phone calls from faraway places were always 'reverse charges'. I can hear the various operators now. 'Mr Kent is calling you from Belfast. Will you accept the call?' It was always yes from my father or mother. Out of that magic circle of family security their two deaths were pushing me.

In some way I had always felt that growing up was something that happened in the future. Even at the age of nearly sixty-five I am still unsure whether the process has been completed. The departure of my parents launched me into a world for which no one is ever really ready. It is the world of being grown up – of not having some other circle into which one can retreat except the circle one makes for oneself. It also means accepting that all dreams are not going to turn into reality. That others are going to take over where you left off and that, after all, you are not going to be Pope or Prime Minister. My father was very fond of two bits of advice. The first was 'Make friends on the way up. You meet them all again on the way down.' The second was shorter: 'Clogs to clogs in three generations.' Both made their own sense and conveyed his feelings about the transitory nature of life as he knew it.

Moreover, with their deaths I have certainly become much more tribal. When the family furniture was finally divided up I wanted little and could not wait to send to the auctioneer whatever the rest of the family did not ask for. Perhaps there should be a law to prevent such immediate post-death rash behaviour.

More and more, as years passed, I began to want the pieces of furniture around which family life had centred for so long. I was able to get back the old dining-room table which for perhaps thirty years had brought us together. It is now my desk and underneath it at one end is the electric bell-push with which my father would summon attention from the kitchen. My mother's old dresser, where she kept her best bits of silver, is now our dresser and gleams with polished wood as it did in her day. I have a box downstairs in which I keep all the old Michelin maps which took my father around France in the immediate post-war years. Both their old-fashioned fountain pens now roll around in one of my drawers. I seem to need these physical links with times past. The priest who, rather rudely, refused me will not know how much he hurt me when he would not sell me a candlestick, no longer in use, which my mother had given to his church. It had her name on it.

These mementoes, like family photographs, connect me with the history of my tribe. So do certain places. On the few return trips I have been able to make to Canada I always go to see the places where my parents grew up, to meet my cousins, to talk over old times, to wonder why those now dead did this or that. Not long ago my brother found the diary which my father had kept throughout his First World War years until he was badly wounded in 1917 at Vimy. He kept all the drama out of it. It is mostly about friends, outings, the horses he rode and the Chinese meals he enjoyed when training in Canada, but at the end of every daily entry is the number of the psalm he said before he went to bed. He never told us anything about those years. I wish he had. He did once say that he was brought on a stretcher to Charing Cross Station and then taken across the road to the old Charing Cross Hospital. I still see that journey every time I go down the Strand.

Perhaps the most recent tribal episode was the search for great-grandfather's grave. We knew that my father's father had left for Canada at the turn of the century. It was my brother who discovered that great-grandfather, at one time coachman to the Duke of Leeds, was buried in Abney Park cemetery only a couple of miles from where my wife and I now live. It took three trips with an axe to the over-grown jungle of Abney Park cemetery to find the grave. But eventually we did. The stone just said: GEORGE KENT. 1896. THY WILL BE DONE. We had been reconnected. Is this nostalgic interest in family history everyone's experience? I don't know. It has certainly become a powerful part of my experience since the death of my parents.

There is more to it than that. I realise now that I also want to imitate. I enjoy being my mother's son. No one could go up our road without a word from her. She knew the postmen, the plumbers, the grocers and the policemen. She fed the nuns who went begging for their orphanages through the comfortable streets of Hampstead Garden Suburb. She seemed to know everyone. Towards the end of his life my father used to say rather sadly, 'How is it that you know the entire street and I don't know anyone?' The answer was that he really wasn't terribly interested in other people's lives, but she was. So am I. Is this imitation or just the shape of the genes? Who knows, but I like being like her.

I also like being like him. He was a good leader. In the old-fashioned, rather paternalistic way, he ran a good company. He cared about his workers, though that did not extend to any sympathy for their trade unions. He could encourage and inspire the people who worked for him. He was a popular managing director, though towards the end rather a lazy one. Too much time spent in the bridge circle of Clement's Club, that rather elite Bush House drinking society, then the haunt of many a City businessman. I liked being like him – getting to the point, making decisions, cutting through red tape, being accessible to everyone, as I was in the organisation where I spent some critical years as general secretary: the Campaign for Nuclear Disarmament.

It is not only in the matter of working style that I find myself imitating him. I like short haircuts and am as regular at the barber's as he ever was. He was rarely late for anything. I have tried to make that my reputation also. Unlike him, I do not turn nasty, just rather loud and silly, when I have had too much to drink. But knocking back whisky would be as much my habit as it was his if I had the money to make that possible. I like method and order. So did he. He liked finding his way to strange places with a variety of maps. So do I. He enjoyed showing visitors around odd corners of London. My interest also. He carefully and regularly cut his nails and took good care of his feet. I do just that.

Again, is all this genes, or is it conscious imitation? I don't know. I do know that there are times when both of them are very present to me. It is not that I have messages or hear voices. I just think of them as about somewhere and concerned. She I imagine as I last remember her – an old lady of eighty, slightly scatty, with a good sense of humour and a lively smile. He as a businessman in his sixties, in his suit sitting at his desk, which now happens to be my wife's desk. Behind one of its drawers not so long ago I found an old, unpaid demand for rates from Finchley Borough Council. Since I assume the envelope got lost it must have been the one and only time that Finchley had to remind Kenneth Kent to pay. He liked paying his bills promptly. So do I.

There is another aspect to this curious partial separation. I keep trying to measure the space of their lives against the space of mine. Now I am nearly sixty-five. When my father was sixty-five he had already been made to accept early retirement by the American owners of the company, who had other ideas about progress and efficiency. When he was sixty-five in 1964 I thought of him as an old man. My mother was desperate to find him something to do that would keep him busy during his retirement but she never succeeded. His interests – family, grandchildren and horses – were not going to be supplemented if he could help it with prison visiting or any other good works. Now that I am sixty-five I understand how he felt at sixty-five. He certainly couldn't have felt old.

Sometimes I think of our evacuation to Canada. Two or three times he flew out to Montreal on government business during the war. Now I realise that he was only in his early forties. I was forty-three at the start of an eight-year span as a university chaplain and felt very young indeed. But when he came to Canada I was twelve or thirteen and in my eyes he was already old. No wonder we do not communicate across the generations. In our heads we remain what we were. In our bodies other people see us change. What did he think, I sometimes now wonder, of his rather opinionated, aggressively Catholic son of sixteen or seventeen? He was under fifty when I was confidently explaining to him why the Pope was the Vicar of Christ and how Protestants had sold out on the one true faith.

There are time comparisons I also make with my mother. At thirty-nine she had to gather up her young family, leave her husband, and cross the Atlantic, already full of submarines, at the start of a war which might have ended very differently. At thirty-nine, at a period which seems years and years ago now, I was in my mind a very young priest in Biafra during a civil war which most people have now forgotten but which had dramatic effects on my life.

These age comparisons help me to understand what they might have felt about their experiences. Now there is a kind of retrospective compassion and concern which I did not feel at the time. After all, they were 'grown up', and grown-ups do not have anxieties and insecurities. Experience has taught me otherwise.

I have also learned how fast it all goes. By the average lifespan of my parents and their brothers and sisters if I last until I am eighty I will have had more than an average innings. That means just another fifteen years. What is fifteen years? Backwards it would take me rapidly to 1979 when I was just about to start as general secretary of CND. Those years have raced past. I can remember the details of them as if they were yesterday. Perhaps fifteen years is over-generous. My father after all died at the age of seventy-three. Only nine more years. It has all gone so fast: whatever happened to middle age?

Not that I have any kind of Dylan Thomas emotions. I am certainly not raging against the dark. As a matter of fact I have very little concern or anxiety about an afterlife. As I get less dogmatic about catechetical certainties I get more sure that all we now see and experience can only be the shadows on the wall. St Paul was right. Now we see through a glass darkly. One day we will see face to face.

Does this mean some celestial tea-party at which I will catch up with my parents' news and wear a wristwatch marked aeons and epochs instead of hours and minutes? I very much doubt it. My image is rather different. Put a magnifying glass up to the sun and redirect some rays. They have such power they can set paper on fire. Reflect the same rays back in a mirror to the sun and they seem to disappear.

We came from the light and we go back to the light. That is quite enough for me.

Meanwhile I count concerned and loving parents as a blessing in whatever form I am to see them again. When they died I had, as is the Catholic custom, prayer cards made with their photographs and dates of death. On hers there were some words from the Apocalypse: 'The Lord God shall wipe away all tears from their eyes . . .' On his are the words taken from the funeral service as the coffin leaves the church: 'May angels lead you into paradise.' Both were good selections, I continue to think.

SALLY VINCENT

Nothing But Contempt

My brother and his wife wore red roses in their buttonholes at my father's cremation. The other ten – she must have bought the full dozen – were strewn on the bottom-of-the-range coffin. Red roses for love. I'd have pinned one on my coat if they'd offered it to me, or maybe held it in my hand just to be different. But they kept their gesture to themselves. I never loved my father, they knew that. This family doesn't go in for hypocrisy.

They weren't on speaking terms. She'd been *supposed* to ring me up to tell me the old man had died because he was far too upset. She hadn't been supposed to blurt out all the stuff about how I'd been cut out of the will and how it'd be better for all concerned if I stayed away from the funeral. She'd only wanted to spare me (she said) the humiliation of the Great Nemesis scene round the dining-room table, with Alastair Sim reading out the last will and ostracism. Life has been one long British B movie for her. Silly bitch. So she wore her rose and her it's-nothing-to-do-with-me face and he asked the undertaker how much he owed him even before we trooped into the chapel. Nobody else came.

I always thought that when my father was dead and buried I'd probably dig him up and jump on his head. I often said so, anyway. In the event I felt rather more ambivalent. Certainly I was determined to pay my last respects, whatever they turned out to be. And I also wanted something cathartic to happen, something that would allow me to emerge a free, fearless, fatherless woman. But the box was too small for such a big ambition: the thunderous finality of the moment nothing against the poignancy of the ridiculous smallness of the box. We stood there in our cold and trivial conflicts and muttered the Twenty-Third Psalm with the duty-vicar and watched as the short curtain jerked across its rod till we couldn't see the heartbreaking little box any more. And all I could think was Christ, how sad. Poor, sad old bugger.

I drove straight back home to London afterwards, my absent mother having expressed through the eager auspices of my sister-in-law a wish not to have me anywhere near her. I wondered, admittedly with very little curiosity, what she was being so vehemently elusive about. Perhaps it was simply that she no longer had anything to impart to me. There was rarely much between us that was not predicated upon her dislike of her husband and the direct implication that I was, in some poisonously visceral way, responsible for his faults. Long after I cared any more I went on trying to reorganise the onus, inventing banal motives for his behaviour and counselling divorce or endurance as her only alternative. But she knew I was missing the point. The last time I saw her she complained, in a desultory fashion, about the shortcomings of their bathroom plumbing. She'd wake up every morning, apparently, and pray not to have to hear it rumble into activity because it meant he was up and about and had failed, yet again, to die in the night. Then, as if this wasn't unpleasant enough, he'd bring her a cup of tea, lukewarm and slopped in the saucer in order to make her feel sick. And she shuddered that theatrical shudder of hers, the one she reserved for spiders and black people.

All the way home from the ceremony of the sad box, I made a conscious effort to occupy my mind with innocuous thoughts of my father. I didn't hope for comfort, just something pleasant to clinch the unexpected sadness. Sorting through my childhood memories I know exactly where to look for the happy ones. I have them stored like snapshots. I even remember taking them. The euphoria would come over me and I'd recognise it for what it was. Yes, yes, this is it. This is happiness. Have it. Keep it. Remember it for ever. I have a field with a brown horse in it, an empty cowshed, a bit of sky, a bottle of Tizer and a hot cross bun in a paper bag and another bit of sky with sea underneath it. And I have these other ones that aren't pictorial, of me running and running and knowing in an ecstacy of certainty that I am so tireless I need never stop; me inside a flat, white, impregnable body, knowing exactly what the stars were for. There's nothing with a daddy in it though; not that I kept.

I did the obvious thing and pictured him laughing. He often made himself laugh till his eyes watered and his lips dragged off his teeth like an astronaut's at G-force times three, while the anguish of a terrible, helpless isolation glinted in his eyes. I am very much afraid that this is what I look like when I laugh and the fear fills me with self-loathing. Safer to remember the back of his head when he drove the old, black Ford Anglia and John and I were little and playing had-you-last in the back seat. We'd be chugging along in second gear astride the white line in the middle of the road. 'This is quite fast enough for anyone,' he'd say as the tooting jam behind us tail-backed into infinity. 'Go on!' he'd bawl when someone dared to accelerate round us, their passengers gawping in our window with slack-jawed wonderment. 'Go on! Bloody well kill yourselves.' This makes me wheeze and choke and my eyes stream. I have to keep my lips tight shut in case my teeth show.

Back further than that, I can remember him as solid and solemn with a foot bigger than my whole leg. Once upon a time my daddy was invincible. My daddy was brave. My daddy was famed for being seen strolling sedately across Chelsea Bridge at the height of a German air raid while all about him scurried for cover. 'Why run with the fox when you can hunt with the hounds,' he used to say in what I took to be the voice of innate superiority. And when the doodle-bugs came we stood *en famille* at the window of our flat and looked down on the timid souls who scuttled across the courtyard to the basement bomb shelters. 'The common herd,' he called them, and we'd back him up like billy-o, jeering at their clothes and panic. Then he'd make us all stand in the cupboard next to the coal cellar to wait for the all-clear siren, and smack our faces in the dark if we giggled. My daddy knew how to keep us safe. My daddy also had a real gun, a relic from the First World War, with which he planned to shoot us all dead when the Germans came clattering up our stairs to take us away. Mummy confided this to us, lest we feared he would fail to protect us to the bitter end.

In all the years I knew him I never had a conversation with my father. Nor have I ever heard him converse with anyone else. He opined, issued statements, monologued. He brought the tips of his fingers and thumb together to make a little tulip shape to wag under your nose. 'The thing is this, you see,' he'd say, and give you the benefit of his mind. I know how complicated his feelings about Oscar Wilde were and how incredibly uncomplicated his views on everything else: homosexuality, socialism, women, ethnic minorities, unemployment, crime and punishment, education, religion, modern youth, art, music, humour and the royal family. It was as though he thought in long, declamatory sentences that would come tumbling out at the approach of a pair of ears. Once, left alone with a husband of mine, he talked for an hour and a quarter about the importance of his feet and their relationship with boracic powder and Elastoplast. At the end of it he motioned as if to whip off his sock to demonstrate how, even as he spoke, he wore a fine example of the latter upon his very heel. At the time I was slightly miffed that I had missed this intimacy. I wouldn't have minded hearing about his feet. It might have brought us together, somehow, as the neurotic eczema had when I was adolescent and he was a young man and we both had to wear gloves all the time. It gave me a sense of belonging, even though I wasn't allowed to use his ointment. In those days, 'You take after your

father' was worth hearing, given that nobody within my earshot ques-
tioned his high opinion of himself. It was only later, much later, that
it meant I was a bringer of grief and disappointment.

When I was very small – before I was ten years old – there was
something we did together. He'd unlock the glass-fronted bookcase,
extract *Palgrave's Golden Treasury,* select a poem for me to learn off by
heart and instruct me in the art of recitation. All I had to do was fix
'Oh, to be in England', or 'I wandered lonely as a cloud' in my head,
which wasn't difficult, and then I'd have to stand in front of him and
say it, making my voice go up at commas, down at full stops and keep
it dead level for all other punctuation except question marks, when it
had to go up more than at commas. The other rule, which I did find
hard, was the one about pronouncing vowels in the northern fashion:
Path not parth, dance not darnce and so forth. This did not come easily to a cockney child, but it was that or a smacked face for my own
good. Anyway, when he judged me to be word and intonation perfect
he'd somehow arrange for me to give a public performance at school.
It says something for the deep and abiding generosity of five hundred
snot-nosed London kids that they didn't shred me after one of my 'I
remember, I remember' shows, but they didn't. Not that I feared
they might; I was too terrified that my father would find out I'd said
parth and darnce.

In those days I managed to harbour a vague idea that he approved
of me, no doubt based on the fact that he never denied the consensus
that I resembled him. At the appropriate time I exhibited my inherited superiority and won a scholarship to a posh school in
Westminster called the Greycoat Hospital. What actually happened
was that I passed the eleven-plus like everybody else but my parents
chose to exercise their claim on the education system by ticking the
Greycoat Hospital box on the presumption that it was the esoteric
thing to do. You had to go along there and be looked at and do a few
tests, but there was no scholarship. Nobody paid to go there.
However, having thus distinguished myself, nothing was too good for

my father's daughter and the occasion was to be celebrated by our first and last outing together. He was to take me, personally, to the enchanted empire of Harrods, there to purchase the symbolic grey coat which would, of course, be fashioned from Harris tweed, a fabric believed by him to possess peerless qualities of beauty and durability.

As we walked down Walton Street towards the back entrance of the great store, I rehearsed ways I could tell him the truth. Look, I know this sounds silly but . . . You're not going to believe this but . . . The grey Harris tweed number was on my back and buttoned to the chin before I had the guts to tell him the school uniform overcoat was navy blue. I wasn't sure he heard me, but he started to move in slow motion. Got out his chequebook, wrote the cheque, thanked the saleswoman, picked up the Harrods bag with the grey totem inside it. Then the long, slow, silent walk homewards. As he ranted to my mother I remember her sighing contentedly and chucking her chin as though they were now fully united in the knowledge of the cross she had to bear. 'She's mad!' he bawled. 'She showed me up, leaping about demanding scarlet coats and emerald green coats and bright yellow coats like some bloody nigger's kid.' He vowed then never, ever, as long as he lived, to buy me another garment. And he kept his word. Nor did I ever forget that I had spoiled the precious father–daughter moment, rejected his pride in me, rubbished the tender gesture and forfeited all hope of familial complicity for ever.

I'd been at the posh school for a year before he relented enough to address me on the matter of my academic career. He opened the school magazine and enquired which form I was in. I told him. Lower four one. Right, he said turning the pages. Lower. Four. One. He found whatever he was looking for and, fixing me with one of his more deeply meaningful stares, pronounced three names. Anne Bailey. Meaningful stare. Betty Smith. Meaningful stare. Sheila Evans. Meaningful stare. I waited. 'These,' he intoned, 'are the girls to watch out for!' He closed the magazine. 'Watch them!' I should have left it at that, but I lacked the diplomacy to understand he didn't wish to be told that Anne Bailey, Betty Smith and Sheila Evans were the prizewinning stars of last year's Lower Fourth exam results and were beyond my personal vigilance as they were now in the Upper Fourth. I had time to flinch as he smacked me crisply across the face. I had been insolent. I had sneered at him. And, having scorned his object lesson in academic competitiveness, I had rendered myself unworthy of future attention. You can't tell her anything, he warned the world. She knows it all. Don't listen to her, she only read it in a book, she doesn't really mean it. Getting something from a book was phoney. If you wanted to know something – really know something – you were supposed to ask him. And he didn't get it from a book. His wisdom was innate.

I think he waited his whole life for me to go to him as a proper daughter should. To ask humbly for the benefit of his experience, to sit at his feet and be guided by his authority. But I never did. We passed each other in the night, my father and I, like two drifting battleships with their radar systems out of whack. His disappointment in me must have been fairly epic as the scholarship girl of his short burst of enthusiasm was transcended by the sullen teenager for whom anything that cost money would be too good and would therefore be wasted. He gradually developed the theory that I was 'unnatural', and certainly nothing that passed between us in those years could be confused with the sentiments normally associated with fathers and daughters. When I think back to his view of me it could only have been of a tight-lipped, tearless child with No written all over its face.

The weeping came later. I don't know what triggered it. Perhaps it was some sort of retarded defence mechanism, a sudden gushing emergence of vulnerability like the one that suddenly and unaccountably consumed me when men indecently exposed themselves to me on the street. One day I was equal to them; they were merely part of the entertainment of London life, rude clowns you could deflate by going up to them and asking if they had the right time, mister. And the next time it happens you're terrified, your heart pounds and your cheeks burn with shame. That was how it was with my response to my father's wrath. One day I was impassive, the next I was a wall of snot and tears against the all-controlling, all-defining rage of the mentor. I was a sodden barricade against his ambition for me. I was to learn to be a shorthand-typist. That was the thing, you see. But he didn't hit me that time. 'You?' he shrieked, his face purpling. 'You a journalist? What makes you think you're so special? There are two hundred of you up the Wembley High Street every Saturday afternoon.'

In one way I almost welcomed these outbreaks of hostility as a way of raising the temperature between my parents. After a good bellowing they somehow warmed to each other as though nominating an enemy gave them something mutual to cherish. It seemed the least I could do. I knew that once, long ago, they had been happy together. In her dressing-table drawer my mother kept a love letter from my father, written when my brother was born. 'Is he a greedy boy then?' it said. 'Does he gobble up all his dinner, just like his daddy?' I often got it out and read it over again, wondering what had happened to the loving couple whose joy in their first-born was hidden under the lace hankies and sanitary towels. The dark secret lay somewhere in the absence of a companion missive commemorating my own arrival two years later. It had to be my fault; the fault of my existence. It could only be the fact of my life that destroyed the real mummy and daddy and replaced them with two cold and spiritless adults whose unity could only be manifested through the sharing of contempt for someone or something outside themselves. It seemed reasonable that the someone had to be me.

I knew, in a wordless, feral kind of way, that I was unwelcome. At night I dreamed I was lost in unfamiliar territory, desperately searching for home. Over and over again, night after night, I came to our front door, opened it and found myself among angry strangers and alien armchairs. But awake I was on my guard: elbows out, intrusive, being there with a vengeance. I'd come home from school full of words to be unleashed into my mother's ears. As I came into the house I'd hear her sigh and the rustle of her bag of liquorice allsorts as she pushed it behind her cushion. Then her feet would come down off the mantelpiece and she'd snap shut her medical romance library book. And I'd be upon her. I'd sit across from her and tell her things. I told her there was no Adam and Eve. I told her eternity went both ways. I told her humanity was a footnote on the great geological chart of recorded life. I told her there was definitely no God. I bullied her with my tongue till she clapped her hands to her ears and went on clapping so she couldn't hear me any more.

I was eleven years old when she told me, as part of a birds and bees lecture on the inadvisability of sexual intercourse, how hard she had tried to dislodge me from her womb and how, 'trust you, you clung like a leech'. It might have been then that I contracted the fear of pregnancy that stayed with me until the invention of the pill replaced it with the comforting guarantee of barrenness. But the part of me that took in the information felt no pain. I rather fancied she admired my tenacity and I empathised with her plight. I already knew she hated girls. I thought it must have been really rotten for her, getting lumbered with a female leech. Really, really rotten. She was my mummy and I was sorry. I also loved her, almost to distraction. When I was old enough to feel the first pangs of sentience, it was the prospect of her death, not my own, that made me sweat in the small hours. I was on her side. I grew up to deplore demonstrations of affection – touching, cuddling, kissing, that sort of thing. 'We are not,' my mother would say in her Queen Mary voice, 'We are not a demonstrative family.' With a father who went berserk and smashed his head on the wall when a midge bit him, or the carving knife ran into a meat skewer, this was a curious assertion, but the cool rectitude of her delivery impressed me. People who touched each other ran with the herd.

My mother and father called each other by their Christian names.
I never saw them embrace. When prevailed upon they would talk
about their childhoods a little, always very carefully and only in terms
of the total correctness, propriety and grace of their backgrounds.
Everything in their respective gardens had been lovely, why was I asking? What was the matter with me? Why must I dig and delve, dig
and delve into everything? Why couldn't I just be happy, like other
girls?

Certain anomalies in their accounts of themselves were obvious,
even to a ten-year-old. My father's siblings were all old enough to be
his parents, for instance, while my mother's sisters were glamorous
and insouciant women who 'spoiled' their children with embarrassingly vulgar displays of physical passion. From my elderly maiden
aunts I learned that my paternal grandmother had been a woman of
tyrannical respectability who had gone quite batty with rage when
she became pregnant with my father at the age of fifty. The aged
aunts had been grown up and working in shops from which they
returned home to be locked in their rooms for the night. Their only
respite from their gruelling life of enforced spinsterhood had been the
advent of their beautiful baby brother. And from my lovely young
aunts I heard tales of a drunken gambler, my mother's father, who lost
the family fortune to the bookies and controlled his brood of fillies
with a horse-whip. It excited me to picture my parents' childhoods.
The mad Mrs Rochester figure fuming in her attic while the pale,
cowed sisters worshipped at the Dauphin's crib. I didn't have to
imagine my mother's past as it was already encapsulated in a photograph in my grandmother's house: a quintet of sweet peas with
apprehensive eyes and entwined arms and my mother in the middle
of the bunch, her mouth compressed unprettily in denial of the
shadow behind the door.

I wondered how such disparate and secretive hearts as my parents'
came to recognise each other and reconcile themselves to the con-
struct of their marriage. The box-brownie snapshot of their wedding

day shows a young couple negotiating the steps outside an east London church, their bodies turned away from each other. My mother's face is blackened by the shade of a broad-brimmed hat, her dress is dark-striped and she is carrying a bunch of what look like tiger lilies. The photograph was not stuck in the family album, which belonged to my father and ceased to catalogue events beyond 1930 when my mother came on his scene. But there was a picture of him sitting in a deckchair holding a parasol over the head of a pretty girl and smiling a smile of relaxed sweetness that might or might not have been a trick of the light. My mother told me she was a friend of his who had died. She mentioned a disease – TB, I think – using the tone of voice she employed for naming just deserts. I filed the information along with the unconventional wedding picture and came up with five. He'd been married before. He nearly escaped his destiny, but she died. So that was it.

My mother, with her customary candour, said she married him because he was a good provider, a responsible husband and father. She never spoke about love, only duty. His to her and hers to him. He had only to raise his hand, she would say, raising hers in clarification, and there would be his laundry. His shirts ironed, his underpants re-elasticised, his socks darned and paired. When he came home his high-protein tea would be on the table, the linoleum polished, the surfaces dustless, the beds made. And in return he would give her a bundle of pound notes each week, to be secreted under the carpet of their bedroom and eked out as housekeeping money.

When they became parents there was no need for them to invent Truby King because one or other of them had either read his book or enough of the excerpts in the *Readers' Digest* to reassure them of the rectitude of their convictions. My parents' version of the Truby King dictat was concise and to the point. Babies want attention. What they need, however, is discipline. You show them who's boss. A crying baby was trying it on and should be ignored, or as my mother put it, 'studiously' ignored. She believed that the intelligence to know when it was hungry was twinned in a baby's mind with the knowledge of when it wanted to open its bowels. Nappies, she concluded, were the recourse of a lazy mother. You feed a baby at X o'clock, whether it likes it or not and you tie it to a pot at Y o'clock, and if everybody followed suit the world wouldn't be in the mess it is in today.

My parents enjoyed recounting tales of their unlazy parenthood till the end of their days. They had a particular relish for repeating an incident from my babyhood. I was only two, apparently, and already displaying symptoms of the waywardness that was to become legendary. Put your toys away, they said. No, I said, bold as brass. Put your toys away or we'll throw your best doll on the fire. No, I said, standing there, arms akimbo, daring them with my eyes. So – and this is the part they loved to tell – they threw the doll on the fire. And Oh my, how I screamed! They were never more united than when they went through the doll-in-the-fire routine. There, said their peacefulness, we kept the faith, didn't we? We were not people to put up with any old nonsense, neither did we issue idle threats. We were better than our word.

I have no conscious memory of this particular conflagration, though my subsequent use of dolls suggests it probably did happen, more or less as described. I cannot remember any 'best' doll, but I can recall two china characters, one big and one small. Pat and Wendy. They sat on my bed with their eyelids at half mast and their stiff little arms outstretched and their proper little frocks pulled down to their toes, waiting for me to be moved by childish frustration – stepping on a hopscotch line, dropping a ball at two-balls – to smack their faces till my hands stung. And while I smacked them I cursed them with all the foul words I had accrued in my seven years to heaven. You blasted – crack – filthy – slap – dirty – wallop – little – thump – *cow.*

I can't help myself. I slide backwards to the more familiar territory of the little pink bedroom when Daddy first pasted up the bobbly pink paper. I am in bed. I have bronchitis again. Mummy brings me a slice of bread with butter on it. The butter is yellow. Wonderfully yellow. The wall is wonderfully pink. I want to see the wonderful yellow up against the wonderful pink. Mummy comes in, screams and runs out again. Daddy sprints in from the bathroom, still in his underpants and with lather on his lips. I'm standing on the bed, rigid, right next to the grease stain. You blasted – crack – filthy – slap – dirty – wallop – little – thump – *cow.*

Why do I tell this miserable story? Why have I told it so often? Why does anyone keep repeating anything unless they hope their narrative will suddenly start to tell itself differently? If I tell it again will it only be a malicious lie I am telling, or a bad dream, or one of those things they call a false memory? But I still loathe the smell of Palmolive shaving soap. It depresses me and makes me feel tired. If I concentrate on the Palmolive I do not have to know that what I'm most tired of is being a bloody victim; of rattling around in the victim's polar confines of hope and fear. Hoping I'm wrong, fearing I'm hopelessly right.

Long after I left their house, I retained an optimism that I could somehow reconcile my adult life with my childhood and gain loving parents into the bargain. When I had homes of my own my best hope centred on having them as guests, as though if they witnessed my autonomy inside my own world they would back off just far enough to see me through other eyes and recognise somebody halfway tolerable. But my homes made them desperately uncomfortable and it was sad to watch them struggling to find expression for their discomfort. My mother ran her hands along skirting boards, looked at her dirty fingers and said 'slut' to herself. My father sat on the edge of a chair, furiously brushing imaginary specks from his trouser legs. He said he wouldn't mind so much if only the pictures on my walls had colour in them. He didn't say what it was he wouldn't mind so much and it seemed imprudent to ask.

I was thirty-nine years old before I nipped him in a budding tantrum and asked him what it was about me that made him so fantastically angry. He welcomed the opportunity. Winding himself up with a few rounds of *you – you* – people like *you* . . . ruining this country . . . *you* . . . *you* . . . *you* . . . You go out on the street, he said, focusing in on the white heart of his rage, you just *go out* and *raise your arm*. You go out and raise your arm and stop a taxi. What, I asked as quietly as I could, should I do? The veins stood out on his head, the glasses jumped on their coasters, the napkin rings rolled off the table. WALK! he screamed. Bloody well walk bloody well walk bloody well walk.

In the course of their very long lives, my mother and father demonstrated to my acute dissatisfaction that people do not change as they get older, they merely become more and more exaggerated versions of themselves. My father became smaller and more doll-like in appearance, his rages became more bizarre and the esteem in which he held himself grew more reverent as he aged. He'd sit in his special, Peter Jones, best-that-money-can-buy-against-which-all-other-seating-arrangements-pale chair, holding himself tenderly by the wrist as he checked his pulse on the stopwatch he kept for the purpose. Whenever I visited him he would take me on a guided tour of his furniture, telling me how much he paid for each item and how much more it was worth even as he spoke. A few hours of my company would usually produce an attack of *you* . . . *you* . . . apoplexy, after which he would carry on with the verbal inventory of his value system as though nothing had happened.

Having foresworn the need for friendships in their younger days, their retirement gave them time to hone the rules of their relationship without recourse to outside intervention. On Sunday mornings they liked to stand at their sitting-room window to watch the village people returning home from church. They knew everyone by sight, well enough at any rate to enumerate the various pious hypocrisies that must have characterised their recent worship. In the evenings they watched television. They had a small black-and-white set to show their disapproval and kept it inside a walnut commode with sliding doors so as not to spoil the room. When their programme was over, each would shut his or her side of the unit and, before going up to bed, each would open one side of the window curtains. If one of them bored of television before the other, the door-closing, curtain-opening routine would still be scrupulously observed. They seemed to be quite happy about it.

No, I was not a good daughter. I did not often visit my ageing parents as they soldiered together through their ninth decade. In fact I hardly visited them at all. I knew that one day they would die and I would be sorry I had failed to please them. I carried on imagining that one day I would prevail upon the seemingly immutable coldness of the familial scene and we'd all live happily ever after. And then they were dead. First the old man, peacefully in his sleep. Then, a month later, my mother died, presumably from her frequently declared determination to do so.

My father's lawyer sent me a copy of his will. It was a perfectly reasonable testament, leaving his entire estate, such as it was, to my brother. There was no need for the codicil.

It was addressed, as these curious documents are, 'To whom it may concern' and neatly typed out by my father on seven pages of quarto a year before he died. This is my father's version of the story of my life. His truth. He began: 'She was always a difficult child' and proceeded through the somewhat banal minutiae of my existence: the rebellious schoolgirl grew up, became a journalist, got married, got divorced, voted Labour, bought things in shops, espoused feminism, had male friends, earned a living, laughed loudly, smoked, rode in taxis, came for Christmas bearing gifts, and so on. I can't imagine who he thought would be concerned by this catalogue – the Queen, the Lord Chief Justice or God Almighty – but whoever it was my father was clearly confident that they would share with him his conviction that my record merited not only disinheritance, but a sizeable stretch in Broadmoor. On the bottom of each page he had prevailed upon my mother to append her signature and the whole caboodle had been witnessed by a fine collection of neighbours who I like to think gained small sherrys for their pains. To fill up the final page, my mother had written in her loopy, familiar handwriting, 'I agree with every word my husband has said. She has nothing but contempt for us.' And she signed her name one last time.

So that was it. My mother often told me I had been born with my eyes wide open. She said the first thing I did was look her up and down and count the cost of her garments. That was her truth. We don't change. Not that much.

My father's codicil tells me nothing I didn't already know and everything I never wanted to believe. He has reached out from the grave and tipped me the wink. No hope. No fear. You can't get a better legacy than that.

SHUSHA GUPPY

Love is All

'Love is all, it gives all and it takes all'
Søren Kierkegaard

I t was around nine o'clock in the morning, and I was alone in the
house. I had accompanied my two sons, aged eight and nine, to the
French Lycée in South Kensington, a mile away, and had walked back
home to start the day's work. The telephone rang – I remember hearing three rings before reaching it. A woman's voice announced that
she was calling from the Iranian Embassy and would I hold on while
she connected me. The voice that spoke was that of Mr Amirian, the
cultural and press counsellor.

I had met Mr Amirian several times before in connection with
work: I had written long reportages for the *Sunday Telegraph Magazine*
since the late 1960s. I had gone to Persia for them to cover the late
Shah's coronation, and again in the early 1970s to accompany the
Bakhtiari tribes during their six weeks' spring migration from winter quarters by the Persian Gulf to summer pastures high in the
Zagros Mountains near Isfahan. And these assignments had enabled
me to take my two small children to visit my parents in Teheran,
which I would otherwise have been unable to afford. I constantly
looked for ideas that would secure me commissions 'at home', and Mr

Amirian had been helpful with information and required documentation. But I had not seen him for a year or more, and in the meanwhile my life had changed radically: my marriage had broken up, and – finding myself alone and having to earn a living – I had signed a contract with a record company and started singing professionally, as well as writing freelance. I shelved a book I had started to write (and which I completed and published fifteen years later) while I grappled with my new circumstances.

What could Mr Amirian want?

After the usual exchange of greetings, he asked, 'Have you heard from your family?' I said that I had not for a week or so, adding anxiously, 'Has anything happened?' A moment's silence . . . my heart was pounding like the amplified ticking of a clock in a horror movie, as if breaking down my chest to escape.

'Well . . . yes . . . Your father. I'm sorry . . . a great man . . . the end of an era . . . a loss to the world . . .' But his voice had receded. I was falling down the shaft of a deep dark well.

I crouched by the telephone and sobbed, clutching my stomach, like the victim of a knife attack trying to close a cut and stop the bleeding. How many hours passed before I moved? I can't remember – the memory of the pain has obliterated any sense of time. I have forgotten the day, the season, the weather, even the year. To find out, last night I telephoned my eldest brother, now living in Washington, DC: 'It was in March 1974,' he said. 'I have forgotten the exact date.'

Could it really be twenty years ago? Whenever I think of the occasion, it seems like yesterday – the same stab, the same *déchirure*.

So the event I had feared as far back as I could recall, and the fear of which in some ways had determined the course of my life, had finally taken place. A recurrent nightmare along the years, this time I was awake and there was no escape. My beloved father, through whom I had first experienced the glory and grief of Love, was gone, and I was alone, thousands of miles from my mother, brothers and sister, my vast extended family of aunts, uncles, cousins, friends – all those who could share and assuage my sorrow, and most of whom would doubt-less be assembled in our house in Teheran at that moment.

What could I do? I wanted to rush to the Lycée, take my children home and hug them with that same anxious intensity with which I had loved my father as a child, and which I had transferred to my sons since they were born.

Only they could console me with their presence and their sweet-ness. But I did not wish to bewilder them while I was in such a distraught state.

I tried to ring our house in Teheran – I still remember the num-ber – but a recorded voice kept repeating, 'All lines to the country you require are engaged, please try later.' A new and enlarged tele-phone system was being installed, and meanwhile it was hopelessly difficult to get through during office hours. The telephone was the lifeline of the many foreign companies and their Iranian counterparts who were scrambling to secure business in the unprecedented period of prosperity and business confidence ushered in by the boom in oil prices. This was the zenith of the late Shah's reign and Persia had become a rich and important player in international politics and commerce . . .

Eventually a kind operator heard my urgent appeal and connected me on a special line, and for a few minutes I could mourn with my mother and my eldest brother. The house was full of people – I could hear voices in the background. How I wished to be with them! But what could I do with the children? Who could I leave them with? And there was my workload, on which we depended for our living.

In the light of what happened subsequently, I now know that I should have found a way of flying out, preferably with the children, if only for a few days. I did not know how essential it was to see, touch, feel, go through the process of mourning in order to heal – that otherwise the loss remains lodged in the soul like a bullet in a wound.

I learned that my father had died in his sleep, two days earlier, of old age – he was ninety-three – 'like a candle that has burnt itself out', and that he had been buried according to his wishes as quickly as his funeral could be arranged. Islam recommends that the body be 'returned to earth' without delay (Muslim burial does not include the coffin, which is used only for conveyance), so that the soul can be truly released and soar to be united with God. I remembered my father explaining this to me once. I envisaged vividly the funeral in detail, as if it were happening before my eyes: 'God is great,' they would murmur as they carried his coffin out and through the crowd of people. 'If you chance upon a body being carried to the cemetery, you walk seven steps behind, to show God your acceptance of your own death and your submission to His will,' they say. Then they bury the body amid prayers, tributes, and the chanting of the Qur'ān and of mystic poetry. Had I been there to participate, this experience would in time have become a sacred memory. Instead, the image of it haunts my imagination and fills me with guilt, for ever.

As in all traditional societies the ceremonies of mourning in Persia, precisely codified and sanctioned by long observance, are deeply rooted in social custom, and enshrined in religion. For three days after a death friends and family call to present their condolences – close family members stay in the house for a week. Black coffee is served with dates and halva – a special fortifying sweetmeat made with flour, butter and sugar – while lunch and dinner are provided for those who choose to stay, and food is distributed to the poor of the neighbourhood, who in return pray for the salvation of the departed. Cantors are called in to chant verses on the passions of saints and martyrs, and on the eve of the seventh day everyone returns to the graveside, which is usually in the grounds of a shrine. There prayers are performed anew, poetry is chanted by cantors, quantities of fruit and sweetmeats are handed out and consumed. Then the crowd disperses, to reassemble on the fortieth day after the death for another visit to the grave, with more distribution of alms and food, and repeated prayers.

Thereafter friends and relations call in periodically to give support and provide company – to console the bereaved is a religious duty on a par with visiting the sick and assisting the poor – until the first anniversary has passed and the loss has been assimilated. To be alone in loss is considered too cruel a fate to be inflicted upon anyone.

I was alone. What is more I had been given the news by a stranger, on the telephone. This could never have happened in Persia – you did not announce death abruptly, through a machine; you prepared the bereaved for the shock with solicitude and affection, with preliminary words of wisdom as to the inevitability of our end, with poems on the transience of the material world, the brevity of human life and the promise of eternity: 'Verily we are from God and to Him we return,' to quote the Holy Qur'ān. Mr Amirian's telephone call was a reminder that I had forsaken these customs of my forebears, and so forfeited my rights to delicate behaviour – I had married an Englishman and become a European, perceived as being tougher, less emotional. How could he know that the truth is often the opposite, that exile exacerbates sensibility and renders more fragile, as a tree with shallow roots is more vulnerable to the weather?

It is said that a drowning person sees his or her whole life in a few seconds before losing consciousness. So it seems with the loss of a parent – suddenly the past unfolds like a scroll imprinted with memories, from childhood to the present. Grief heightens self-awareness, as if a torch were conducted through the darker recesses of the soul, revealing long-hidden reserves of guilt, remorse, sorrow. Albert Camus once wrote: 'the love of a son for his mother constitutes his entire universe'. So it was in my relation to my father – he was the centre of my life from the beginning of memory, and I loved him with an intense and painful passion. Once when I was five and we were spending the summer in the country, my father went to Teheran for a few days on an urgent matter, and I pined for him so much that I fell ill, with swollen glands and fever. A friend of his, a doctor on holiday, was called in. 'You should not let this child be so attached to you,' he later told him, having diagnosed the nature of my illness.

My father had married late, and I was the last of his four children – two boys and two girls – so that he was already in his late fifties when I was a small child. His hair and beard were turning grey, and sometimes grown-ups talking among themselves would remark that he was getting old. Children have an acute sense of logic, and in my mind old age was associated with death: had not his brother Hashem and his stepmother Amineh, both only a few years older than him, died already? So perhaps he would too? The thought was unbearable. Sometimes I would burst into tears 'without reason', rush to his study upstairs, and tell him that I was afraid he might die. He would be infinitely gentle, promising that he would live for many, many years to come, and that I had nothing to worry about. He would sit me by his side, hold my hand and resume his reading. If I went into his room and found him asleep, I would listen to his breathing to be reassured he was still alive. We know that parents are anxious for their children, but we don't always realise how much children worry over their parents – he clearly understood and tried to soothe.

As I grew older and my world became larger through school, and contact with people outside our circle of family and friends, my love for my father did not diminish, but I became aware of him as a public figure: everywhere I went, at the mention of my surname people asked whether I was related to 'The Professor', and when I said that I was his daughter, a stream of superlatives gushed forth in his praise. Older people who had known him for a long time would recount anecdotes and stories illustrating his knowledge and wisdom, his integrity and humour, his spirituality and tolerance. I began to realise that the gentle old man in the study, surrounded by piles of books that sometimes hid him from view, was a philosopher and sage loved and venerated by everyone, high or humble. If this was a source of pride, it also created obligations: 'How could the daughter of such a man do anything so naughty?', or obtain anything but the best marks?

I wanted to know more about my father. We had no pictorial record of his youth, save for a sepia photograph taken when he was about twenty, which my mother had framed and kept in her room: a grave young man with intense dark eyes and fine features, an icon. Since he never spoke about himself I quizzed my Aunt Ashraf (his younger sister by four years), who stayed with us for long periods, as well as my mother and other members of our family, to learn about his past. Gradually it emerged.

Born towards the end of the last century, my father had been both witness and actor in the historical upheavals that had transformed Persia from a crumbling empire into a modern state. As a young student he had been caught up in the Constitutional Revolution of 1905, in which his own father and some of his teachers were among the leaders – progressive mullahs who had sided with modernity, democracy and change. Later, when Reza Shah founded his Pahlavi dynasty and tried to haul Persia into the modern world, he was called in to supervise the creation of a new Civil Code based on the Code Napoléon, and to ensure that it did not clash with Islamic principles – which would have provoked the wrath of the clergy. Finally he was appointed a founding member of the Royal Academy and given the chair of philosophy at the University of Teheran – the first Western-style university in the country, which gathered its intellectual elite and became a prototype for other such foundations in Persia. By the time I was born he was already a national figure.

This was my father's professional history, and was well known. By contrast Aunt Ashraf's chronicle of our family was woven with miracles, dreams, edifying proverbs and aphoristic verses, often illustrating the immutability of human destiny: 'Our struggles are the agitation of a straw in a turbulent sea – which thinks it is causing the waves, not just being tossed about by them!' And she would shake her head with disdain. She regarded my father, whom she had worshipped since childhood, as an example of Divine Grace, and of God's direct hand in individual destinies: 'The nightingale lays seven eggs, but when they hatch only one becomes a nightingale, the others are just starlings,' she would quote, an old proverb. 'Your grandfather produced eight children, and your father, his third son, was the Chosen One.'

She would then proceed to tell me about his *Riazat* —the tribulations, hardships and suffering attendant upon the life of a Seeker-after-Truth. 'Those whom God loves, He tries,' went another proverb. It was years of *Riazat* and asceticism, allied to constant prayer, fasting and meditation, that endowed a person with the 'Third Eye' – with which you saw deep into the human heart and far into the future – and with the 'Healing Hand' – with which you took pain away from the body and torment from the soul. This was as true of my father, she believed, as of the saints and Sufi masters of the past, about whom she was a treasure-trove of stories and anecdotes; or the Indian yogis who occasionally came all the way from the East to see my father. (One of them arrived when I was born and predicted that my life would be lived far, far away.)

My father's *Riazat* had begun when he had lost his mother at the age of five, and he himself had nearly perished by catching fire while playing with some matches. His father, a high-ranking mullah and well-known theologian, presided over a large, indeed munificent household, but neglected his children. They were left in the *Andaroon* (the women's quarter), until they grew up. My grandfather was not ambitious for his offspring, perhaps because he had achieved eminence himself: he married away his daughters at the ages of twelve or thirteen to the first man who asked for their hands, and his sons at seventeen or eighteen, 'as soon as a soft down shadowed their upper lips', just to get rid of them. Only my father broke the pattern: 'He took himself to the local school, and began to earn his living as soon as he could read and write, by teaching others and writing for the unlettered, so as to be independent,' explained Aunt Ashraf.

Later he had gone to the Polytechnic College, established by an enlightened nineteenth-century vizier and modelled on its French counterpart in Paris. While studying philosophy, he taught mathematics to support himself; and after graduation went on from one *madrasah* (college) and its various teachers to another for twenty years, not only in Persia, but in the Middle East and Europe as well, studying the traditional curriculum of philosophy, logic, theology, canonic law, astronomy, mathematics and medicine. 'By the time he came back, he was already over forty and his reputation had preceded him,' concluded his sister.

He had never wished to marry; he intended to lead the contemplative life of a Sufi and philosopher, living in one room at a college. In *The Genealogy of Morals* Nietzsche points out that the great philosophers were seldom married, the notable exceptions being Socrates, whose union with Xanthippe was an expression of his irony, and Hegel, who married 'through absent-mindedness'. I once mentioned this to my father and asked which of these descriptions fitted him. 'Both!', he said jokingly. We teased my mother by referring to her as 'the Professor's absent-mindedness'. Visiting an old monastery in France many years later, I was reminded of him, reflecting that he would have been perfectly happy living in such a place. In the event he was chivvied into marriage by my maternal grandfather, a forceful jurist and judge who, captivated by his charm and knowledge, persuaded him to take his daughter, whose suitors he had hitherto refused as unworthy.

Marriage meant earning a proper living. He could have opted for a meteoric career in the religious hierarchy and become a Grand Ayatollah, but his kingdom was not of this world – power and its compromises did not appeal to him, while the life of academe allowed for detachment. In later years he was offered a seat in the Upper House (the Senate), ministerial portfolios, chancellorships of universities, religious leaderships – all manner of high office – but he refused them all. The exercise of power clouds the soul and hardens the heart, and he did not want it. He himself never told us about these offers, and we learned about them only through the newspapers and friends. Yet he was tolerant of ambition in others, and constantly pulled strings to help them.

As a child I knew nothing of all this, nor of his philosophy. I was just a daddy-worshipping little girl, quivering with pity and fear of losing a frail old love-object. Later I learned that he belonged to the school of Illuminationists, Islamic Neoplatonists who since the thirteenth century had sought the fusion of Islam, Greek philosophy and Zoroastrianism. But he wore his learning lightly, laced his lectures with anecdotes and jokes, softened his irony with benevolence, and as a result his lectures were widely popular, and many came to hear him from as far afield as Japan, India and Europe. 'Until the very end, when he was so frail and weak that he could hardly speak, he still tried to joke and tease and amuse visitors, so that it was not a chore for them to come and see him,' my mother told me after his death.

As the pace of modernisation and Westernisation accelerated, it was not easy for a traditional family such as ours to keep pace. By the time I was born, Reza Shah had abolished the veil and decreed the emancipation of women – of all his reforms the most controversial, the most toughly resisted by the clergy. My parents had to negotiate a tricky course between moving with the times as they wanted, and keeping their traditional ways in order to reassure those who relied on them as guardians of values. My sister and I were sent to school, but we were not allowed the freedom our friends enjoyed – dancing, singing, joining the Girl Scouts, and country outings were forbidden. I resented such infringements upon my freedom, and turned against religion, the cause of these restrictions. Indeed, as all four of us children gradually stopped practising, my mother fretted and feared for our souls. '*You* tell them – they will listen to you,' I heard her say to my father. But he was far-seeing and knew that coercion would only turn such a passing rebelliousness into a permanent phobia. And indeed each of us found our own way back to a spiritual path.

A suitable role in life for me would have been marriage to an upper-class young man, perhaps a diplomat or in government, who would rise to the top of his career – and this was what happened to my older sister. Alternatively, being a bluestocking, I might prefer not to marry at all but become an academic. But I wanted to be Casting Director of my own life – myself. I was ambitious for freedom, knowledge, adventure, love.

The only solution was escape – to go to Europe where women were truly free!

The only drawback was separation from my parents. How could I live without my father, who always put everything right, brought problems down to a rational level, consoled away disappointments? A few months before I left a cabinet minister came to visit him, and as he was leaving he turned to me and said, 'You are going to Europe in pursuit of knowledge? All the knowledge you need is in this room.' But I knew that I had to find my own way, as my father had done himself.

Yet did I ever leave? 'Nothing, ever, takes away our childhood,' wrote Simone de Beauvoir about her mother's death, in *Une Mort très douce*. You take your traumas, your illusions with you wherever you go: 'You can't run away from yourself, Jack!': the shot freezes, the fugitive from justice stops in his tracks. And so, away from home I looked for surrogate fathers, and was lucky to find one or two.

More problematically, I believed my father to be a paragon of intelligence, goodness, *grandeur d'âme*, and unconsciously sought the same. I was disappointed when other men fell short. 'My dear Mademoiselle, if you go on like this you'll never marry!' warned my French doctor. 'Every little girl thinks her father is perfection incarnate,' he went on, dismissing my protestations. In the end the biological imperative prevailed, and I gave up the pursuit of the ideal, though I remained susceptible to certain qualities: because my father was attractive and charming, I was fatally attracted to men who had charm and good looks; and as he was trustworthy, I trusted them. I did not know that charm is often a social device 'turned on' for personal gain. As my father never lied, I believed everything I was told, and was often deceived.

*

So there I was, sitting by the telephone and mourning my father, alone. When my sons returned from school I explained to them that I was sad because my father, their grandfather, had died. 'But you will never die, will you?' I reassured them that I would not, for a very, very long time, and that they had nothing to worry about . . .

It took two years before I managed to go to Persia, see my mother, and visit my father's grave. One night after everyone had gone to bed and the house was quiet, I went into his study. It was left untouched, and everything was in its place, as if he had just gone out for a few minutes and would be back if I waited. Even the familiar smell – of clean linen, rosewater, waterpipe tobacco and old books – clung to the air. I sat on his mattress for a few minutes of reflection, my heart breaking with nostalgia and regret, missing him. I remembered how in the past sometimes the room would be full of visitors, conversation and laughter. Presently one of his students who had a ravishing voice would start singing mystic love poetry by Rumi, Hafez, Khayyam. 'Come, Cup-bearer, and pour forth the wine/For Love seemed easy at first, then proved fraught with difficulties . . .' I used to sit beside him as a child and enjoy it all, until at the age of ten I was considered grown up, and barred from men's gatherings. From then on I listened from the adjoining room, as I loved the singing. I remembered the sound of his steps as he walked along the corridors and rooms at night, murmuring prayers and putting out our lights when we had fallen asleep over our books . . . Sometimes I would wake up and hear him chanting the Qur'ān and the Midnight Prayer, and would be moved to tears by the beauty and pathos of his voice . . .

I then understood that I had left home all those years ago to run away from his death, and that all other reasoning had been a cover-up for my cowardice, my inability to face what I knew to be inevitable.

Next morning I was happy to wake up 'at home' – if my father had gone, my mother was there, my aunt, the old staff, all of whom I loved tenderly. The structure of our family life was still intact, with my mother as always at its centre. For if my father had set the tone of our life, it was my mother who had 'managed' it, 'run the show'. Besides, my love for my father was not some Oedipal obsession that excluded my mother. On the contrary, I adored her too, but she was young and beautiful, and I took her for granted. I did not associate her with death – she was life itself, with her energy and gaiety, her gift for friendship and capacity for love. She had married at eighteen a man twenty-three years her senior, whom she had never seen until her wedding night. Yet he had charmed her, and she had fallen in love with him, once and for all. She had no formal education, but my father had encouraged her to cultivate her artistic talents – she designed our garden, trained the cooks, beautified our home. She was a natural hostess and entertained family and friends unstintingly – the house was always full. And all on a professor's meagre salary.

She became more and more pious as she grew older, until in the end nearly all her time was spent in prayer – she simply moved from her prayer-rug to her bed at night and back again in the morning. She believed that it was women's task to pray for everyone, especially for the young who were too busy to do it for themselves. She prayed for her children, her friends, the world.

When the Revolution came in 1978–79, her world was shattered. In the exodus that followed, those who had been involved in the administration of the country under the Shah, including my eldest brother and my sister, went into exile (my younger brother, an artist, and I had always lived in Europe). Her house was occupied by 'revolutionaries', including young relatives of old servants, who claimed 'their right' to her property and possessions. And none of us was there to defend her – we were all in danger of at the very least imprisonment if we ventured back into the country.

All these turmoils – the loss of her children who would perhaps never be able to return, the occupation of her house – finally took their toll, and she became suddenly old, with loss of memory, arthritis, heart trouble. She died eighteen months later, and this time I was given the news by my sister in person, and we mourned her together. I heard that permission had been refused to bury her with my father in his mausoleum, but that a kind cousin had given his own 'allotment' nearby, in the grounds of the Shrine, which solved the problem. Then we heard that the house had been 'bought' by an entrepreneur, who had pulled it down and built six other, smaller houses in its place. The few photographs that I had taken of it and brought with me to England are all that remains of it. I have framed a coloured picture of our garden – the blue pool, the tall pines and their birds' nests, the flowerbeds.

Nowadays I miss my mother more often than my father. Perhaps because he had such spiritual reserves that the absence of his children did not affect him as much as it did my mother. She had a pagan soul, despite her religious faith, and her children were her entire life. 'All I want is that my children and grandchildren be around me when I'm dying,' she once said. None was. Instead revolution raged and shattered her world. 'It was her heart – she went quickly and painlessly,' my aunt explained. I owe my mother my freedom and my work. It was she who insisted that my sister and I go to school, have a modern education, and be able to earn our living if need be: 'Who knows what the future holds? Whoever she married, saint or tyrant, in future a woman should be able to fall back on her own resources and earn her own living. Otherwise she would be a slave.' Those views were in advance of her time and upbringing, but she knew instinctively how society was changing.

Revolutionary tyrannies seek to destroy memory, as a means of control, so that new generations can have no reference to the past, no criteria, says Anna Akhmatova in Lydia Chukovskaya's *Conversation with Anna Akhmatova*. What is left of our family except our personal memories? Must they fade and vanish with our lives? My father would have been horrified by the revolution and its aftermath.

Ironically, the leader of the revolution, Ayatollah Khomeini, had once attended his courses on the esoteric doctrines of Islam and Sufism!

Much has been written about the psychological burden on their children of having distinguished parents. When I arrived in Paris I realised how relative fame is: no one except a few specialists in his field knew my father, and I was just an anonymous student like thousands of others. Yet he had left me a moral and spiritual example as hard to forget as it is to emulate – sanctity is not a matter of inheritance, but of Grace. I have long given up trying to live up to my parents' astringent standards, but they induce guilt and remorse whenever I fall short.

Time does not heal loss – you just learn to live with it. After the shock of bereavement and mourning one ceases to think of people one loves as 'dead' – they just seem absent, out of reach, and acutely missed. During the day preoccupations push aside the sadness of loss, but in sleep at night the psyche is exposed. In my recurrent dreams my father is sitting by the pool in our garden, dressed in his white robes, smiling and happy. By contrast, my mother is lost amidst the ruins of our house, and I'm looking for her, walking through broken masonry and glass, muddy puddles and jagged walls, until in the end I find her alone in a back room, as if waiting to be rescued. It does not take a psychologist to understand the meaning of these dreams . . .

One of the shibboleths of our age is to deny regrets – even politicians who do not speak French quote Edith Piaf's song 'Je ne regrette rien' when they leave office! Yet regret is a natural and authentic human emotion: we all feel it at times. Perhaps the only thing not to regret is the profligate expenditure of emotions, including regret, which is what the song means, and which is the source of creativity. I regret sorely not having spent more time with my parents while they were alive, not having realised that their love was more selfless and pure than any I could ever again find or earn. 'It is all in the order of things: human clay is kneaded with loss' – I can almost hear Aunt Ashraf quote, from Heaven.

DEBORAH MULHEARN

Shortness of Breath

It always puzzles me when people say so and so looked in death exactly as they had in life. My dad looked nothing like the person I knew. I was so convinced I was looking at the wrong body in the funeral parlour that I went back to the receptionist to check. She pointed out the name on the upended coffin lid and said they had never had any complaints. I said I wasn't complaining, it just didn't look like my dad. I brought my sister back the next morning for a second opinion. I was offended by the tawdry coffin, the changed features and papery skin, the cheap white lining tucked around his face so you couldn't see his still abundant hair, and the gruesome lid waiting to obliterate him completely. I pulled out a wisp of hair and we giggled with relief.

It's been a struggle to write about my dad. Even though I have a fairly fixed image of him, the flux of feelings sees him shift and fade from view so that every time I thought I could begin, I immediately felt I hadn't even begun to touch on my real emotions. The only certain thing I knew was that the bag of bones sealed in that coffin was not him. So if that wasn't him, where was he? What was he? Who was he? The cold division of death has little relevance. I was his daughter and I loved him, but I can't say I miss him, which is odd because he pervaded my life and up to this point still does. I can't say

I think about him a lot, but my dybbuk-dad is deeply entrenched. I loved him madly when I was young, and when it palled with the pull of the outside world, he punished me with subtle blackmail, telling me family was all you needed. So it's no good wondering why his dying didn't free me, for me he lives and pulls the strings. Perhaps being dead makes it even easier for him, now he hasn't got his own life to lead.

He didn't realise all this of course, and didn't want it to be this way. He wasn't malevolent, and it's crashingly obvious to me now that the special bond I thought existed, stretching right back to my birth which he witnessed, was at most resisted and more probably a figment of my girl-eager imagination. I don't even think he liked me. I think of him affectionately, a small man ruffled by a big world, his soft face incongruous in a hospital bed, bereft of light and hope and the ruddy cheer that set him square against the world.

Just after he died, a friend asked me if I felt guilty because our tense relationship had ended unresolved. I didn't, and two and a half years on there is still no backlash. This has puzzled me, as I feel guilty about virtually everything else, and I know at times I put up barriers of my own. But it struck me only recently that I was the child in that relationship, and he had a responsibility for my happiness which he reneged on. I don't know what he felt; I only know that in the end, the final month when he was in hospital and roles were rudely reversed, it was too late.

My grief at the time and afterwards was largely for my mum, for her loss and their loss. I had lost him long ago, it seems. And the sharp intermittent pangs that came, at places which reminded me of him, or full family times like weddings and Christmas, were for him not me, because he lost his life, and as a family and individually, we had to see and feel those moments and memories for him, as if my mum commanded it, from her prickly throne of grief.

I remember the irrational childish terror at the thought of your parents dying. It gripped me again when he took ill, but dissipated when it seemed he would get better. Then he sank again and the last four days when he lost consciousness dripped by in an emotionless vigil, stirred into relief, not fear, by his death. I thought he would die in the bleak hours before dawn, but he pushed on uselessly till tea-time. So it was a noisy, peremptory affair, with all of us crowded into the stuffy side room of a busy hospital ward, with everyone outside knowing why we were in there, and clattering their teacups regard-less.

He died from a stroke at the age of sixty-four, and it seemed des-perately unfair, because he was a young sixty-four, on the threshold of a happy third age, active and boyishly enthusiastic, with his children and attendant traumas behind him. The blow of not reaching sixty-five was bitter. Skewed by shock, we thought of him as a man cut down in his prime. Happy people don't die. It wasn't until after a brain scan that we realised just how massive a stroke it had been, and that it was quite incredible that he had survived it at all. A less fit man, a smoker or drinker, would have died straight away, the doctors told us, and we wondered whether it would have been better if he had not survived. My mum said she lost him that day. He had suffered a mild stroke a week or so before, and had dismissed it with customary gallows humour. Privately he must have been terrified, and glimpsed God knows what horrors.

When the big one came, it was the early hours and my mum could only hold her convulsing husband helplessly until it stopped and the ambulance came. Early-morning or late-night phone calls still make me jump. I drove to the hospital, a new driver in a still unfamiliar car, jolting and stalling at every junction, not knowing if he would still be alive when I got there. Eventually we reclaimed him, stretchered and awaiting transfer to the ward. He was pale and weary from the huge physical trauma, but conscious and so relieved to see us. In those few serene moments I saw the last of my dad as I knew him. For the next month he was babied, cajoled and comforted, wound slowly down to the end of his life. At first he rallied, started physiotherapy and talked about weekend visits home. I was constantly searching for signs of duplicity in the doctors and nurses, any outsider who saw things more realistically and wasn't tricked by the stealthy deceit of hope. My mum talked about rearranging rooms at home to care for him, and I half wished away such a burden. He never saw his home again. He lived for a month and a day through restless days and dream-heavy nights. The stroke stripped much of his manhood away, exposing a truculent child.

We came and went, wife and seven children, satellites around his sunless body, not quite believing he could die, not quite expecting him to live. The night before he died, the nurse had shooed out extraneous members of his ridiculously large family, saying we were starving him of oxygen. This grisly irony made me think of his own retort whenever asked what someone had died of: shortness of breath.

Tinker, tailor, soldier, sailor. This father-love has cost me dear. I never saw him alone in hospital. Once I hung back and said, I love you, and told him not to worry because we were looking after Mum. He nodded, eyes averted, maybe inferring the worst because why else would I assert this? As a young girl I gushed sentiment all over him, but as an adult that easy expression was stifled. There was no getting to him. There was no chink in the armour of their unassailable bond. As I saw it, he nurtured his relationships with his 'good' children, and withheld from the wayward ones, in the case of my older sister killing it off completely because she outraged his Catholic sensibilities by having a baby before she was married. I strained and faltered. I didn't know what to do with the mess of my love. I was already estranged. And then, at the end, I tried to focus it by being there, forcing myself to watch his bewilderment, his decline. I would have nursed him, would have done anything. But I wasn't needed. I was the bumptious daughter whose presence jarred.

There was one extraordinary day, his last day of consciousness. Up until then he had chafed and fretted in his bed-prison, talking endlessly of petty things that were worrying him. All that went on that last day. He was playful and winsome like a happy drunk. I went in with my mum and he kept saying how much he loved her, how amazing she was, repeating thirty-eight years, thirty-eight years, and pursing his lips to be kissed. This childlike calm was initially reassuring, but then it dawned on me that some layer of his consciousness was telling him the end had come. The nurse told me that he had called my name after we had gone. I know it was because he was muddled in time and thought I was still there, and that it was only some daft thing he wanted to tell me. Nothing deep or significant, he just called for me, and I wasn't there.

Then he went into a coma, and the only sign that he was still there was a return squeeze of the hand if I squeezed his. That gradually weakened, and even this gentle commune was wrenched away by a doctor telling me it was just a muscular reaction. In the night I badgered the nurse. Did she think he would die? Do people come out of comas this deep? Was there any point in hoping? Nurses are more forthright than doctors, but if I had listened to what I heard I would not have let in hope. Then a doctor stood at the end of his bed and shook her head, saying, 'Such a young man, such a shame.' This was the first unequivocal indication that he was dying. I saw it register on my mum's upturned face, and recoiled at the brutal dismissal of my protestations that there was still a chance he would wake up. 'Oh, no, not now,' she said.

After that I still kept vigil, but I had abandoned him. It took a couple more days for his lungs to drown. I sat up two nights on the run, unnecessarily because there were others there, but I wanted to be there when he died. At home, my boyfriend held our baby out to me, saying, 'She needs you', but I was far away. My mum touched my wayward hair once, uncharacteristically close, with some gentle reprimand to do something with it. Her implacable strength saw him out. I was impatient to end the ordeal, and showed it callously, asking why couldn't he hurry up? The nurse took me outside and told me off; it was impossible to be sure he couldn't hear me. I was outraged and mortified. The doctors had talked about him in the past tense, here was some stranger telling me I was unfeeling. My own father's deathbed! How could I say such a thing? How dare she tell me what I could or couldn't say! Only I could be so tactless.

Now here was my father's death, and the impossibility of ever making a connection, and myself, just one of seven, divisible, heard but not listened to, outlandish and undignified, shouting, 'He's gone to Grandpa, he's gone to Grandpa' quite involuntarily and quite inappropriately as father and son had never been close. I was half struck by the irony of them dying on the same date, and half relieved to find some serendipity in the whole ignoble business. His head was turned my way, and the end of his life was too public. The disparate lives of my family were pulled together by this most natural event, but somehow it was the gaps that were revealed. We drove home in convoy.

In the desultory days that followed there was a physical closeness, circling my mum's force-field of grief. He had to wait eight days to be buried because of a gravediggers' strike, another indignity I like to think he would have seen the funny side of. Death was a peculiar notion because he was among us, like Jesus in the upper room, perhaps more potently than ever in his actual life. But this presence, for me at least, quickly evaporated. I stood in rooms vainly trying to sense him in some way like my mum obviously did: his voice, his laugh, his singing, his crummy jokes and puns, his face lit up, his face crumpled into a sulk.

At home I was restless and alienated from the daily run of things; at their house I felt redundant and piqued by the activity that excluded me. I tried to obliterate the putrid image that people said would fade, but I had vivid dreams of his body lying next to me, indelible where he was once inviolable. My grief was in abeyance. It seemed paltry next to my mum's desolation. What was there for a daughter to cherish? You can't go through his things like a wife. You can't admit your ambivalence and so you collude in the shock and grief and disbelief. You hear yourself repeating platitudes, more for the comfort of others than yourself. You glide through the funeral, and wonder if any of the two hundred people who sent sympathy cards and crammed into the tiny chapel at the seamen's mission saw him as you did.

He saw me born, I watched him die. I felt close to my dad, felt I understood him. He wasn't an enigma to me like my mum is, but I know I would miss her more if she died. I don't understand why my thin grief didn't match the horror of watching him die. A friend told me of the immense relief she felt when her mother finally admitted that, no, she didn't really like her daughter, just hadn't taken to her. My dad purveyed the myth of the big happy family, but the closeness between him and Mum excluded, even damaged us. Three brothers and three sisters and a legacy of unease softened briefly by his death. After the funeral everyone played cricket in the garden while Mum sat silently watching through the window. But old rivalries and rifts soon reasserted themselves.

We converged at the time of his death, two even uprooting lives in the south to come back to Liverpool. Two and a half years on we are less entangled, slowly establishing lives, jobs, homes, families that previously only my eldest sister had managed to achieve, because she had to. All but one of us lives within walking distance of my mum, but if she died I suspect we would scatter like a diaspora. Sometimes I think I spot him on their local high street, but it's just some other lucky old bastard. I hate to see elderly couples walking hand in hand or arm in arm; I scanned the death columns of the local paper for ages, getting indecent consolation from tragic, untimely deaths and contemptuous of anyone who lived beyond sixty-five. My abiding image is of him sitting waiting for my mum in the foyer of the local Tesco's, ostentatiously reading a copy of the *European*. He used to boast he had been to every country of the world that wasn't landlocked. My five-foot-four colossus, citizen of the world.

MARY STOTT

The Music of Time

It is more than sixty years since my mother died. She was fifty-seven, I was twenty-three. How strangely little I remember of her actual death – she took to her bed on a Saturday night, was pronounced to have pneumonia, and died on the following Thursday. Meanwhile I went to work as usual. It must have been my brother John who told me, for he had a foreboding she would die and kept close to her side. He always had been the closest of us to Mother – perhaps because he had been a very delicate baby and needed her more.

The funeral I can remember fairly well – how as the hearse and mourners' carriages moved slowly down the road to the crematorium every man we passed solemnly raised his hat. But nothing after that. The next day I went back to my job writing a daily women's feature for the *Leicester Mail*, to which my mother had contributed a daily recipe and an occasional paragraph. People must have written to me or spoken to me, expressing their sympathy, but of that I remember nothing. My daily life went on more or less as before – except that I stopped playing the piano.

That was the one enduring, unshakeable bond my mother and I had – music. My relationship with my mother had not always been happy. I worshipped her when I was little, but in adolescence for

some inexplicable reason I felt positively repelled by her, even physically. I am sure this was no more than what we now recognise as a
need for 'space'. Poor Mother wanted to know more of my thoughts
than I could bear to share. Once she asked me why I couldn't or
wouldn't talk to her, and I replied, 'I think I am afraid of you.' We
both burst into tears, but even that did not ease our problem. I am
quite sure that if she had lived until I had been away from home for
a few years we should have been able to talk and share our interests . . . we had so much in common. But at least we went on playing
piano duets, or, more importantly, piano quartets, two people on
each of the two pianos. Whenever we had a piano-playing guest Mum
would seat him/her on a piano stool beside her, and brother John
would be instructed to sit at the other piano with me. John was a vio-
linist, not a pianist, but he had had some piano lessons, enough to be
able to cope, with some help from me. Our favourite work was an
arrangement of a Beethoven septet – which I am still able to play
occasionally with obliging visitors, having acquired a second piano
myself.

For by far the most precious souvenir I have of my mother is her
beautiful Grotrian-Steinweg upright piano. I had not been around to
take charge of my mother's trinkets when she died. I would not allow
anyone to remove her wedding ring before she was cremated (Did one
of the crematorium staff acquire it, I wonder?) and only took away the
turquoise and black onyx ring she was wearing when she died . . .
which I still wear on special occasions. I remember giving each of my
sisters-in-law a brooch and a ring of Mother's, but what happened to
the rest I never knew. It was only a year later when my father died
that the household goods had to be divided among us. My brothers,
both happily married by this time and living in comfortably fur-
nished houses, were willing for whatever I fancied to come to me. I
had the splendid French oak sideboard my maternal grandfather had
given to my mother for a wedding present, the family dining table
and a few of my paternal grandfather's elegant mahogany dining

chairs (which, I am glad to say, are now in use in my daughter's home). But her piano is the possession of my mother's that means most to me. She bought this for £100 – in the later 1920s, I guess. It was a huge sum in those days and my mother had saved it up over the years by hoarding her Co-op divi. I think my brother John coveted it also, and had an idea that my mother intended it for him, but he generously gave way, keeping the inferior second piano for himself.

What else, beside that precious music-making background, did my mother give me? Not domesticity, anyway. I have often felt that the physical strain of so much domestic labour must have been one of the causes of Mother's early death. Those were the days when bed-linen, tablecloths etc. were boiled in a great brick copper above a small coal fire, and then pushed through a wooden-rollered mangle and hung out (in the back yard, in our case) to dry. Everyone then, of course, came home for midday dinner. We had roast lamb or beef on Sundays, and cold meat or mince on other days, fish on Fridays, and hotpot on Saturdays, but always a cooked pudding. Mother was good at boiled suet puddings of every kind, and fruit pies and tarts. (I think my favourite pud was treacle tart.)

Mother did not rate as a first-class cook but she was an assiduous jam-maker, and bottled plums and other fruit, and pickled onions and red cabbage. She also used to make large amounts of chilli beer (rather like stone ginger beer), leaving it to ferment in a great earthenware bowl and then standing the bottles on the back staircase where they often used to explode, blowing out the corks and fountaining the beer down the stairs.

Those were the days when everyone used to be involved in the Christmas cookery, of course, even if it was only giving a stir to the Christmas pudding. Mother would make enough to cover everyone's birthday as well as for the festive season itself. There was one for Dad's birthday in February, one for Mum's in May, mine in July, and John's in September. Not one for Guy, though, because his birthday was only three days after Christmas Day.

My own experience of housewifery was mercifully brief. About a couple of months after Mother died, I was fired. The *Leicester Mail* was teetering on the verge of financial collapse and had to shed staff. I was thought to be an obvious candidate for redundancy – should I not be needed at home, to look after my bereaved father? So I had a taste of what my mother's life as a housewife had involved. After only two or three months my father – who filled in the 1931 Census form entering me not as 'housewife', but as 'journalist, unemployed' – found an advertisement for me in the newspaper trade press for a woman's-page job in Lancashire, for which I applied successfully.

The domestic experience was probably good for me in the long run. Somehow or other I coped with the cooking, cleaning and washing with the aid of a rather dim little maid. (We usually had one maid, always from one of Leicestershire's coalmining villages.)

There was one other important aspect of a female's life my mother did not give me – confidence in my appearance. My brother Guy's wife told me my mother had said I was 'a cross between a heathen Chinee and a monkey'. My eyes were not blue, like my parents' and my brothers', but hazel. Unforgivably to my mother, it seems, my hair was dead straight, without a flicker of a wave or curl. So every night Mum put it in curling rags. No use. The curls fell out after an hour or so, and so for most of my childhood I wore my hair in a pigtail. My hair was so thick that nowadays it would be considered quite an asset – but not for me.

My mother herself was no beauty. Her hair was straight too, and her nose was quite pudgy. I have always been glad to have inherited my father's Roman nose, even though it is rather large, for it is *straight*! The fact is that my mother had a natural charm which I seemed to lack. Nor was I ever encouraged to make the best of my appearance; though looking at childhood photographs it seems to me that at least I had a pleasant smile. I don't think that in my mature years Mum was ever fashion-conscious, though I have an old photograph of her in what may have been her wedding dress with a very nipped-in waist. She used to boast to me that when she was a girl her waist was no more than eighteen inches (mine, even when I was slim, was never less than twenty-six). Of course this tight-lacing did young women no good at all. I often wonder if it did some damage to Mother's lungs and was one reason why she succumbed to pneumonia. As I remember them, her clothes were always simple – except for the first evening dress I saw her wearing after the end of World War I – it was a long black *charmeuse* gown with a diamanté corsage and I thought it quite stunning. Mother's favourite colour for me was pale blue, and I remember the joy a rose-pink hair ribbon gave me when I was staying at my aunt's in Dulwich at the end of the First World War. This visit was because I was supposed to be recovering from a 'nervous breakdown', which had caused me to be found wandering in a rather dazed state on the way to school. It seems clear now that it was unquestionably malnutrition, not nervous tension, that caused my weak condition. Rationing during the war had drastically limited the amount of protein we could have, whether meat, butter or poultry. All our butter ration went to Mother because she was on a diet that excluded meat. We had no cakes or buns and Mum used to make us oatcakes, which I found so disagreeable that I used to slip out from the dining table and flush them down the loo.

What my mother did give me, most importantly, was my career in newspapers. I clearly inherited from both my parents an aptitude for putting words on paper and I had been in and out of the *Leicester Mercury* office with Mum since early childhood. But I owe her more than that. When I quite suddenly made up my mind, as a result of having to write an essay at school on newspapers, that journalism was what I had to do, she not only had the willingness, but also the ability, to open the door for me. She went and talked to the editor of the *Leicester Mail*, a Mr Chandler, and persuaded him to take me on. Rather cleverly he put me into the proof-reading department for a few months, which gave me the 'feel' of the paper. But Mum's brother, my Uncle Harry, must have helped a good deal, I think. My very first day on the *Mail* he came upstairs to the readers' room with a couple of tickets in his hand. 'I want you to cover this concert for me tonight,' he said. (Uncle Harry was not only chief sub-editor but also music critic, art critic and theatre critic!)

So I went to the concert with Mum, and then sat down by the gas fire in what we called her 'writing room'; it was on the way to the bathroom so could not be used as a bedroom. I think I expected to be up all night, but in fact had finished in about an hour, and my little notice of 'Miss Constance Hardcastle's Pupils' Concert' went in, word for word, exactly as I had written it. Both nature and nurture had obviously worked for me.

Within a few months I was moved from the proof-readers' down to the reporters' room where I used to 'make the calls' – going round to the police stations and the fire station to see if there were any incidents to report, and to the market to pick up prices. Quite soon I was allowed to go to inquests and magistrates' courts with a senior reporter, and later on my own. It was a heartbreak for me when I was taken off reporting and landed with the women's column – the end, I feared, of all my hopes to be a real newspaper journalist. But I dare say my mother was quite pleased for me, and I realise now that this experience of attending women's functions, especially the more political ones, interviewing distinguished women – including Mrs Emmeline Pethick Lawrence as well as Sybil Thorndike – gave me a good background for the days when I edited the women's publications of the Co-operative Press, and even for my later *Guardian* days.

I certainly owe largely to my mother my lifelong interest in politics and public affairs. Probably my earliest dateable memory is of riding round in a taxi with my mother, wearing a green ribbon round my hat. That was, I believe, during the general election of 1912, when, obviously, she was campaigning for the Liberal candidate. (Later she campaigned for that distinguished Liberal leader Sir Gordon Hewart, whose wife bought me a dear little baby doll. I thought I ought to call him 'Gordon', but that seemed too solemn for him, and he became Billie – the most precious doll I ever had.)

Another very early memory was presenting a bouquet to a Lady Crewe at a great rally in the Temperance Hall, Leicester. I managed to hand over the flowers successfully but no one had told me what to do then. I stood for a moment bewildered, and then, seeing my dear 'Nunkie' on the far side of the platform, picked up my heels, ran, and leapt into his arms. It must have been a wow! 'Nunkie' was T.W. Smith, at the time an election agent who had come to lodge with us for the duration of the election but remained for a number of years. He was married, but lived apart from his wife, who was a permanent invalid somewhere on the south coast. He was entirely integrated into our family life, and we always set off together in the mornings, he to his office, I to school.

When the family attended the sort of pleasant dinner dances that were customary in those days, 'Nunkie' was always Mum's partner. My father, surprisingly, for he had an innate sense of music, never danced, except once in a way to partner his young daughter in the Lancers! I have often wondered about Mum and 'Nunkie' . . . for he plainly was devoted to her. And though my father and mother seemed always to be the very best of friends, they did not share a bedroom from the time we moved in 1914 to our Highfield Street house, to the time we moved on to Mere Road about a dozen years later. I now believe it was their pathetic method of contraception. When we moved to our last family home Mum would have been past the menopause so she and Dad could once again share a double bed.

It was under my mother's influence, I am sure, that I joined the Young Liberals when I left school, but I was pretty quickly drawn into the Independent Labour Party under the influence of young colleagues on the *Leicester Mail*. During the general election of 1929 I suggested I might put up a poster for the Labour candidate in my bedroom window. Mother was strongly against it, but my father said gently, 'I wouldn't think anything of any young person who did not start on the Left.'

That general election, of course, was the first in which women could vote on the same terms as men, at twenty-one. I had just passed that age, and was immensely proud of being one of the very first female twenty-one-year-olds to register a vote. Strangely, I do not remember my mother rejoicing with me and for me. She was not, in fact, a feminist, though when I had a look at some of her writings in the old *Leicester Mercury* I did find that she would occasionally urge young women readers to be active citizens. Mother was certainly not a suffragette; not even a suffragist like Millicent Garrett Fawcett, I fear.

It seems to me that she must have been like Mrs Humphry Ward – that powerful novelist of the turn of the century who became president of the Women's Anti-Suffrage League – who supported the current 'anti' view that 'women's political incapacity' came principally from 'an excess of sympathy in the mental constitution of women which shuts out from their mind logical power and political impartiality'. Or, as Mrs Ward herself put it, 'the emancipating process has now reached the limits fixed by the physical constitution of women'.

How sad it seems to me now . . . I know my mother had the brains, the capacity, the willpower, to be a member of the Board of Guardians, a city councillor, an MP – even, I believe, a cabinet minister; and I know her brothers thought so too. But – though really she ran the show in our happy home – she actually believed our father was inevitably head of the household. I well remember that when I began work she asked me for a token contribution of five shillings a week to put towards my food. 'It is your father's responsibility to maintain the household,' she said. And indeed Dad did pay all the household bills. Mother's small earnings from the *Leicester Mercury* remained her own, and I am certain she spent most of it on us, her sons and daughter.

Perhaps, in the long run, the most important thing my mother gave me was a profound sense of family. She herself was the oldest of a family of seven – three daughters, four sons. Their father as a lad growing up in Essex scared birds for a living, and said he had had to teach himself the alphabet. My mother's mother came from Rensburg in Schleswig-Holstein, was born a Dane and grew up speaking German (after the German conquest in the 1860s). Family legend has it that when Charlotte Jonsen came to England (probably in the wake of Queen Alexandra, I guess) and disembarked on the Essex coast, William Bates carried her ashore, and fell in love with her! We all called my mother's parents Mutter and Vater, though they reared a very 'English' family. My mother must have been as conscious of owing a great deal to Mutter as I am of my indebtedness to Mum.

For many of the sixty years since my mother died I suffered bitterly from guilt. At the time I had been inextricably involved with a fellow reporter – but through pity rather than love. John D. had been deserted by his wife, who had gone off with their little son – he never saw him again – and had taken to drink. I felt a compulsion to try to rescue him, which naturally greatly upset my mother. Alas I was quite unable to talk to her about it and it was very many years before I could shake off the feeling that it was her anxiety and fear for me that had caused her death.

Now I can look at her old snapshot albums with fond memories and even 'talk to her' mentally. And I still echo the words my mother said sadly to me when Mutter died, well into her eighties, 'It doesn't matter how old your mother is when she dies . . . a basic part of you seems to have gone.'

PETER MARTIN

Riding the Nightmare

My father was a Polish sailor, all heel-clicks and 'I kiss your hand' by way of greeting; my mother, an English war bride with eyes too big for her heart. Zladislaw (Jimmy) met Peggy Rosalie at the Regent Ballroom, Brighton, in 1942.

All I remember of my father – a memory from babyhood – is playing with him and my mother on a bed (in what I identified years later as a bedsitter). The smell of toast done under a gas grill can take me straight back there – he's wearing a vest and trousers; they're laughing; there's no fear.

I must have been coming up for two when my mother heard that my dashing dad, still a-sailoring post-war, had jumped ship and was now in California intent on starting a new life for us there. In the meantime, we lived with her parents, my pop and gran, in their tiny two-up and three-down in Brighton. My Uncle Jack was there, too, for a while; then he married and emigrated to South Africa.

My mother's elder brother, Uncle Bill, was already away and living in Royal Tunbridge Wells. He'd married into the Browne family – the Brownes of Ronuk patent floor polish – which had a nice symmetry because Gran used a lot of Ronuk in her job as a charlady. 'That's Browne with an "e", you know,' she'd say. 'But they're ever so nice.'

I remember Mum and me getting ready to go to America. I was

six, seven. There was a drama about passport photographs, and a great sense of specialness. By way of anticipating our new life, my father had sent me a Roy Rogers cowboy shirt of breathtaking glamour – check and plain, tasselled back and front, enamelled poppers, curved pockets, a good likeness of Roy himself embroidered on one collar point, Trigger on the other. We were to sail from Southampton on the *Queen Mary*.

At the last, we didn't go. After that, whenever a blue airmail letter arrived from America, my grandparents would become furious about 'that *tyke*' – my father – and my mother would shut herself in our bedroom and cry. I'd sit on the landing – anger downstairs, sobbing above – desperate to make it all right, enormous with uselessness.

Whatever it was that had happened, it was clear that my mother still loved my father very much, but she never allowed herself to be unhappy in front of me. She called me her 'sunshine' and brought me big apples from work; bubblegum, too, sometimes, but we kept that between ourselves, knowing my grandparents would regard it as vulgar and, worse, bubblegum being American, as contraband of a daddy-referring sort.

Boy, was my mum proud of me! I *felt* like her 'sunshine'. She had a large-mouthed smile that dinked and flashed all over me. Especially she liked me to go places with her. I have a photo of us, tilted together and beaming, on a summer day at the entrance to Brighton pier. A man with a parrot took it. You can see how brimmingly proud of her I was: that's my mum, that is.

One afternoon, unusually, my grandfather met me from school, steered me into the local park, and said we should sit down. I was nine. 'Mummy's gone to Jesus,' Pop said, stroking the grass. 'She won't be coming home any more.' I'm not sure if the words 'died' or 'dead' were mentioned, but I sort of understood. I was also used to the fact that a lot of what adults said couldn't be fathomed. *We won't be going to America to live with Daddy*. Oh, all right. *Mum won't be coming home any more*. Oh.

Back at home, my grandmother turned her head away, and I noticed she was wearing my mother's favourite necklace. That felt wrong. The house was full of gloomy neighbours. Anxious to get out of there, for this not to be anything to do with me, I asked Pop if I could go swimming. It was an outlandish request, I knew, but I needed somehow to test my standing. *Mum gone?* Where did that leave me? What could I expect from this point on? So out it came: can I go swimming? Best not, Pop said, giving me a look; go and collect the evening paper, and take Derek with you.

Derek, my best friend since we were five, lived a few doors away. He knew already my mother was dead, and more. Making me promise not to tell, he repeated an adult conversation he'd overheard that afternoon – an act of loyalty to me for which, then as now, I feel a solid sense of gratitude. My mother had been found in the kitchen, he said, dressed for work, her head on a pillow in front of the gas oven. That morning, she'd seen everyone out of the house: Pop to work, me to school, Gran to her half-day's charring. Gran had found her. 'Committed suicide' was a phrase Derek had caught. On the way back from our newspaper errand, we discussed it at some length, hanging upside down off some railings.

No adult ever told me how my mother died. Aware that it was dreadful information, however, and not intended for me, not by adults anyway, I determined to let none of them know that I knew. But no adult thought to provide me with any sort of cover story about how my mother had died. So, for anyone who asked – which kids did a lot – I invented my own, basing it on the fact that my mother used to do large amounts of typing and big-ledger accounting. Her brain had burst due to overwork, I'd explain. Kids were grateful to be told and invariably satisfied. There'd have been no looking them in the eye with the whoopsy likes of 'She's gone to Jesus.'

Although we'd all been living in the same tiny house, until Mum's death I'd not experienced my grandparents as anything other than

novelties, sepia-coloured people from another age, background enti-
ties. Now they loomed close, Victorian, stern, musty. When they
announced, rather formally, that they would look after me, the idea
that I needed looking after, coupled with a definite sense that they
might have decided not to undertake the task, was very frightening.

The terms of my tenure were strict. Tears and any mention of my
mother were forbidden. 'You must try to be a good boy,' my grandmother would counsel, 'and not upset your grandfather.' It was a
warning. Pop, with his chronic bronchitis, was easily brought low.
His well-being, and therefore my security, depended on my keeping
my grief to myself. That was the deal, and how the appalling secret
was held intact.

I'd had no warning about what I might feel. The hours before
sleep were the worst. Gran would sometimes appear with a glass of
milk and a sign to keep quiet, as if she'd sneaked past Pop and could-
n't stay long. She'd never cross him.

Much too late I realised that there must have been a funeral, that
there had to be a headstone somewhere, a place where I might see my
mother's name; but I didn't dare ask.

The only adult who'd now and then mention my mother was one
of Derek's aunts, Daw Wickham. She would contrive to tell me, slipping it in like a gorgeous gift, 'She was lovely, your mum.'

But I couldn't let Daw know that I knew of her suicide; so that was
that. In solitary, with all the feel of inhabiting a punishment cell, I
couldn't but conclude that my mother's death had been my fault. I'd
failed to make her happy enough to want to stay alive. I remembered
occasions she'd asked me to go shopping with her, and I'd refused; it
was the only thing she'd asked of me.

I now had a revolving repertoire of nightmares. For its exhausting
persistence, the worst involved the torture of flesh with white-hot
pokers. Whose flesh was never clear; no body parts were discernible.
I seemed to be the torturer and the tortured, sadist and victim. I took
to sleep-walking, too, which was differently frightening because I

couldn't keep these perambulations to myself. You always head straight for the fire, my grandparents told me.

In waking life, I'd search for my mother in familiar places – high street, Brighton promenade, our favourite beach – sometimes glimpsing her, always losing her, as if deliberately. I hoped that whatever life she was leading now, she was happy.

Sometimes, on my way to somewhere else, I'd pass the house where my father, Mum and I had lived in the toast-scented bedsit. I knew which window had been ours. There was no seeing in now for net curtains, but I could look across at what had been our view from the window: two very tall abattoir chimneys which seemed to turn against the sky.

Early on, before the mere mention of my mother became a sure trigger of Pop's wrath, I'd got my grandparents to buy me a budgerigar by telling them she'd promised me one, which she had. It wasn't so much that I wanted a budgie. In the first stage of loss, with its awful sense of infinity, I'd become alarmed by how little of my mother I had in the way of mementoes: the pier photo, a brass piskie from a holiday in Cornwall, and two passport snaps, one of her smiling, the other with her eyes fluttered shut. The budgie had all the significance of a special gift, from her to me, and turned out much more of a joy than I'd imagined: quickly tame, funny, clever.

My grandparents seemed to like me less and less. Back when my mother had been alive, and I'd won a medal in my first school's sports, my grandfather had taken some pleasure in getting it engraved. But now – when I won a ten-shilling prize in a school's exhibition for a clay head or, later, when I got a place at grammar school, as my mother and two uncles had famously done – such things seemed not to count in my favour.

Quickly, it got so my grandfather couldn't bear me. For coming home with my trousers torn or unthinkingly drinking the last of the milk, he'd lecture and rail, each time obliging me to promise I'd try harder, then ridiculing my promise. There seemed to me something diabolical about a man screaming. 'You can never do anything right,' he'd bawl, and it worked exactly like an instruction. According to Pop, there was a correct – i.e. most economical – way to do everything from sharpening a pencil to cleaning shoes to the daily management of a bar of soap (proper uses, drying of, storage).

One Saturday morning he stood over me to check that I was cutting sandwiches in the way he deemed correct, a method predicated on the idea that you could spread marge more thinly on the cut end of a loaf than you could on a slice. You didn't just marge and slice, marge and slice, though, or else each sandwich would come out with one of its slices back to front, which wouldn't do at all. The correct sequence was an alternating one: slice, marge the slice, marge the loaf, slice, slice, marge the slice, marge the loaf, slice . . .

I was used to making sandwiches to take to school but with Pop at my elbow I fell to pieces, as did my every effort. Wrong sequence – 'No, *slice* next!' – and then the bread started to crumble, going into holes with hugely wasteful gobbets of margarine stuck in them . . . Pop screaming . . . my hands and eyes juddering. He wouldn't let me stop.

Pop didn't have to be raging all the time. He could discolour the house with a mood for two, three weeks. Of all his accusations, 'You're just like your father' was the most terrible. What did he mean? What had my father done that was so unspeakable? I had no real idea, nor of the counts on which I apparently resembled him. Consequently, 'You're just like your father' had all the mesmerising power of a curse, obliging me to accept that I was bad in ways that I would never understand. That fitted me well: I *had* caused my mother's death without knowing anywhere near fully how I had.

By way of maximum censure, my grandparents would sometimes wonder aloud – without anger – if they shouldn't send me to a home after all or, less specifically, send me away. Each time, it felt like a mortal threat. Forbidden grief, I seemed not to know that the dreadful had already happened.

At school, I'd already lost face and place, going from unthinking confidence to bullies' victim within a couple of months. So gone-to-nothing already, I had no resistance.

Between home and school, I fled back and forth as slowly as possible, and between times took revenge on the only available victim, my budgerigar. Most days, I'd let it out of its cage, well aware that it would eventually fly at the window, crash, and daze itself; I'd take hold of it then, as if to comfort it, before squeezing until it was struggling, terrified. When I finished junior school, leaving my tormentors behind, I stopped torturing the bird, and gradually it got some of its confidence back, but never enough to fly again. Self-loathing is stressful work.

Pop wouldn't let up and, for about a year, between the ages of eleven and twelve, I subdued myself at home to the point of not speaking unless spoken to: say nothing, be nothing, give him no excuse. My silence was partly protest, but now I think, too, that I'd been dragged from below by serious depression for the first time.

Puzzled, Pop backed off a bit. Then I realised I could talk – say things, anyway, fake a little animation, appear to re-embrace the domestic contract – without giving too much of myself away. I became more adept at heading off Pop's wrath: 'How are you today, Pop?' 'Can I help you with that, Pop?' I was his creep. Before, I hadn't been like that.

More generally, I'd become an old-fashioned creature, polite, so *good*, hair brushed, flannel-shone complexion, concave with apology. The worst kind of adults approved of me. Somewhere along the line I'd discovered in the family album that someone had cut my father's face, very neatly, out of all the wedding photographs.

Within a year of my mother's death, there occurred a small event which meant nothing much at the time. Returning home from the seafront one summer afternoon, I learned that a Victor and Halina Martin – my father's uncle and aunt, who lived in London – had dropped in on my grandparents expressing some sort of concern for me. I'd never heard of these people. Foreign, exotic, and swish with it, apparently, they'd arrived in a large American car bearing flowers and a bottle of wine (for which Pop had had no corkscrew) – an occasion so special that Daw Wickham had been dispatched by bus to the seafront to find me, but hadn't been able to, so I missed them that first time.

The initial excitement waned anyway. Either my grandparents – who mistrusted all Poles – resisted their close interest; or Victor and Halina kept a judicious distance; or both.

My grandparents were born in the 1890s, and both their backgrounds had been a mess of drunkenness, domestic violence, sudden deaths, and the threat of instant destitution. According to Gran, who'd whisper such things to me by way of caution, Pop's resolve never to raise his hand to anyone or to drink (in excess of half a pint of Guinness a week) or to neglect his duty as a husband and father was rooted in that background.

To Pop, everything was an opportunity to economise. All wrapping tissue from the baker's had to be brought home untorn and then sliced into precise squares for lavatory paper. There were people in our street, no names, who used newspaper! Except for his Sunday best, all Pop's trousers had gussets in the seat, usually of a different stripe and colour from the trousers themselves. Other kids had their trousers merely patched or darned; Pop would wholly re-seat mine on the treadle Singer. Oh, he did everything *properly*, and took special delight in the noise of economical labour – stropping his self-sharpening Rolls razor, clack-clack-clack, for ten minutes every evening, smashing away at his boot last as he affixed Philips stick-a-soles out in the yard, as if the bloody glue couldn't do its job properly without his assistance.

Actually, Gran wasn't too much of a dab hand at the domestic disciplines. She knitted very badly and peeled potatoes like a plutocrat, chiefly on account of acute arthritis in her hands; her knees were suety footballs from decades of charring, but she'd never sit down at home of a weekday. Her having gone into 'below-stairs' service at the age of thirteen elided neatly with her idea of house-wifely duty. Pop would now and then 'joke' about the likes of her cavalier potato peeling. But when, last thing, he'd take the coals out of the fire for next day's use, I'd sometimes catch her looking away in small disgust.

As well as being a mean old sod, he was some sort of hero. His thrift was inextricably bound up with other disciplines – duty, sobriety, cleanliness, good manners, and a practical respect for your betters, especially teachers, who controlled the routes to self-advancement. Taken all together, it was this powerful aspiration to decency which had propelled my mother and two uncles into grammar school. It was a remarkable achievement for all concerned – not least because there were no books in the house or anything resembling informed conversation. The assumption that I'd go to grammar school was enough to get me there.

While the neighbours admired my grandfather, they didn't like him much. He'd say hello politely, even warmly, but wouldn't socialise and never invited anyone to the house.

When I was fourteen, Pop asked what I was going to do when I left school, and was infuriated that I'd assumed I'd be taking my O levels at least before making any major decisions. He said he wasn't prepared to support me any longer, produced an RAF recruitment form he'd sent away for, and insisted that I apply. The idea of quitting home and trying to make my own way hadn't occurred to me. The summary nature of Pop's decision had called up an old dread. He wanted rid of me; I went.

When my grandmother died – I was twenty – I felt only the familiar suspension of grief. Mostly by letter – I'd been posted to the Middle East for a year – Pop and I struck up a rather sentimental man-to-man understanding. He told me how proud of me he was; I told him how grateful I was. He'd only ever tried to do what was best, he wrote.

Then Pop fell ill, got better, and married his health visitor, all within eighteen months of Gran's death. Having never seen him so happy, I only wondered at the saccharine versions of our family history his new wife had come by. She was a nice dope. Ask her the time, she'd press on you a leaflet about homoeopathic Christianity.

When he was dying, Pop and I did what we had to manfully enough, our old, avoiding silence intact. The secret of my mother's suicide still lay between us. Sometimes delirious, he'd rant at me like he used to. Had it taken me so long to appreciate his rage and pain? From different angles, I was still the replica of both Jimmy the tyke and his dear Peggy.

Within six weeks of his death, I bought myself out of the RAF, determined in a young man's conceit that I would now live my own life. Set on getting into journalism, I managed to come by a job as a staff writer on a good magazine. You could get that lucky in the late 1960s.

Why had my mother not joined my father in America in 1951? What, at the last, had stopped her from going? I avoided finding out until after my grandfather had died and my old forbidden state had begun to ease slightly. Not that I felt in any conscious need of answers. Aged twenty-three, now my own man and chesty with it, was I not emotionally self-sufficient through years of having to be? Ha! I was bomb-proof! It was as a sort of passive questioner, then, that I let Victor and Halina tell what they knew. Here's the compressed version.

My father had a brother, Stanlisaw (Stanley), who was already set up in California at the time my father sent for my mother and me. Way back in 1943, in Brighton, Stanley had met my mother, and thought a good deal of her. But by 1951 Stanley had become so appalled by my father that he wrote to my mother pleading with her not to come to America. According to Stanley, my father was a wastrel and a drunk who couldn't get himself together, let alone support a wife and child.

Hence, in great part for my sake, it was my mother who had refused to join my father in California. But in a spirit of shooting the messenger — and probably trying to staunch her own hurt at the same time — she'd broken all connections with her Polish relatives, including Victor and Halina.

My father had had a typically dashing-Pole kind of war, escaping from two prison camps, getting across Europe to Britain, then joining the merchant marines by way of doing his bit. Beset by citizenship complications after the war, he jumped ship in Argentina, then headed for California where he'd drifted from job to job — mostly on building sites — making nothing much of anything. A few years after my mother died, he'd remarried, had a son, Phillip (I have a half-brother: oh), but was later kicked out by his wife.

I'd never felt a strong desire to meet my father; I suppose he'd been part of the forbiddenness in me for too long. Besides, even as I was beginning to learn about him from Victor and Halina, I was racketing around trying to sort myself out post-RAF.

Call it bad timing. When I was twenty-six, and the magazine I worked for sent me to America for six weeks, my father had already been dead for two years. In Los Angeles, I visited Stanley. He was very open about all that had happened, about his part in it, and said, despite everything, he couldn't regret warning my mother not to come to America. Otherwise, Stanley was able to tell me only two things I didn't know about my father. For the last years of his life he'd been a golf caddy, on and off, and had died following a three-day bender subsidised by a tip of fifty dollars given to him by Bob Hope.

The other thing was that he'd aspired all his life to be a writer. Perhaps defending against the old curse — 'You're just like your father' — I couldn't think of it as anything other than a touching coincidence. Stanley, who had little idea of the quality of my father's writing, gave me a stack of it – a dozen stories, some going into twenty versions. More than frustration, there's rage in the repetitions; he knew his stories were no good.

Stanley also gave me a photograph of my father, taken a couple of years before he died. Sitting with his feet up, reading, specs on the end of his nose, he's wearing a mohair sweater and his shoes have been mended with stick-a-soles; one is missing.

In so far as my mother had loved me well, I was all right. In so far as I was sitting on top of a mess of unresolved grief, and didn't know it, I was very much not all right, and didn't know it. Women friends recognised me as something of a wooden Indian, emotionally, but that hardly made me much different from the next man.

The first rumblings of trouble, too, seemed merely like a young man's fear of commitment: I tended to end relationships abruptly – two in particular – with near-fits of quick, sullen anger. The only clue to the real nature of these episodes was my pure, hard, justified, bomb-proof afterglow. *Hurt them before they can hurt you?* Whatever it was, it didn't last, and I thought little more about it.

The next episode was more volcanic. I was living with a young woman and as per usual, not fully owning up to my feelings. But as an explanation, fear of commitment no longer felt quite right. I'd protest passionately about all kinds of things, but occasionally she'd give me a sceptical look and I'd suddenly hear my hollow notes.

Anyway, it was a Sunday morning: idle, sensuous, sunny, the whole day still ahead. I was making coffee. The attack was like an eruption of brain lava – a sudden mix of anger, fear and juddering panic so strong, I clasped my head in my hands as if to stop it exploding. Believing it, I insisted this was nothing to do with my girlfriend, and took myself for a walk, afraid of what further harm I might do. A few months on, as if holding down another eruption but giving it full, cold expression, I dismantled the relationship. Just as sentimentality is displacement – feeling about the "wrong" thing – so my anger had felt like that: self-deceiving in a way I couldn't comprehend.

My next relationship – we've been together now for twenty-one years – started with a series of endings, chiefly consisting of me storming out and back to my own flat, head molten, shirts trailing out of my suitcases, and, according to my wife, cricket bat under my arm. Funny about the cricket bat. I'd given it away years before, but my wife swears I was carrying it, as if she'd glimpsed a psychic snapshot of a tantrumy boy. Again: anger about the 'wrong' thing.

Without knowing it, it's very likely I'd been manic-depressive since a boy, but clear into my late twenties the up and down cycles coincided conveniently, if deceptively, with my pattern of work – rushing-about research, the solitary down of writing, the rising high of the final draft, the absurd hilarity of finishing; and around again.

By my mid-thirties, despite my considerable professional experience, each piece of work seemed fractionally more difficult. Writing had never come easily, but I seemed now to be wrestling with large forces of self-prevention. Eventually, the work and depression cycles became increasingly out of synch, and the down-cycles got deeper and longer: three months, six, a year. This, too, would pass, surely. It was like living under water – conversation as muffled sounds, friends irrelevant, work just about impossible, everything slowed to half-speed.

The sole punctuation was the odd attack of molten panic. Desperate to offload it each time, I'd pick quarrels at home, blaming my wife, threatening to pull the bloody house down, damaging our relationship a little more, afterwards finding myself at a deeper level of depression. Then I just stopped, broken down under a weight I could no longer bear.

If it's true that therapy is of no use unless and until the subject is ready to be helped, there was no doubt that I was ready. Very suddenly aware that my life was at stake, I was determined to have help. Bugger all that nonsense about developing a model relationship with the therapist. I used mine hard – mapping out my circuits of repetition, of snuffing the life out of situations for fear of their getting out of my control, unpicking dreams, undermining the old forbiddenness, looking for any way to slip out from under the weight.

But when old, bad stuff is all you know, what other security is there? The therapist said nothing, and I quickly began to hear the crap I was talking. In thundering earnest: 'I like to do things *properly*.' Do shut up, Pop.

I'd told the therapist a considerable number of terrible-grandad stories. But one session, I was nine-tenths through another miserable tale when he started to smile, couldn't contain himself, and burst out laughing. He wasn't supposed to do that. Nobody had ever done that. Over the years, I'd learned that I could paste *anybody* into a corner with my terrible-grandad stories. What could they say about such awfulness? Nothing! There *was* no way out!

But when the shrink laughed, I laughed too. The relief! One moment knees-bent under the burden, the next light-footed and fit for dancing! The terrible-grandad saga *was* like a series of bloody awful, immensely predictable Russian jokes, each with a punchline more miserable than the last, with me as their butt *and* dutiful guardian. And the fraudulent sentimentality of my poor-lad recollections! 'Who can read Little Nell without bursting into laughter?' (Oscar Wilde); or even shades of Monty Python: 'Oh, *we* used to live under a newspaper and Dad'd come home every night and kick us all.'

Just as heartening, once I'd learned that the panic attacks couldn't destroy me, they lessened in intensity and frequency. Now, when I feel a vibration starting up, I can usually step sideways, so to speak, and let the storm roar past. Still, though, I'll sometimes stage a row, and not realise what's happened until afterwards.

What's galling is that there *are* things to be legitimately angry about; but my outbursts are usually fraudulent – about the 'wrong' thing.

After just seventy hours of therapy over eighteen months, I stopped on the grounds that the returns, for which I was still working hard, had diminished to nothing. With the therapist's encouragement, however, I set about an obviously unfinished piece of business: witnesses.

As a boy, my isolation had been almost total because of the lack of candid witnesses. The suicide, the aftermath of grief, the reality of what had happened: all of it had been consigned to silence. As a consequence, I could sometimes doubt my past experience to the point of believing that I was mad or a liar or a large hole in the air.

My one piece of independent testimony from boyhood was Derek saying to me once, unsolicited, 'He's ever so strict, your grandad, isn't he?' – and Derek never said much. It was my one glimpse of the possibility that, whatever had gone wrong, whatever was bad, it might not have been all of my doing; and I'd kept tight hold of it ever since, a talisman.

Now needing to know more, I got in touch with my mother's elder brother, Bill, to whom I'd not spoken since a year or so after my grandfather's funeral. Pleased to get my letter, Bill invited me to visit. It was good to see him. Having come primarily to find out what I could about the unhappy past, but not wishing to frighten him off, I exaggerated the success of my life and times since quitting the RAF, and let the critical topics arise of their own accord.

About Pop's exacting way with money, Bill said of himself: 'I became like it, too, so help me.' At what he said next I felt something like a cramp of recognition: 'I used to save when I couldn't afford to.' A useful piece of corroborating witness, and a welcome touch of kinship.

At another point, making a half-joke of it, I mentioned that I used to be afraid of Pop. Bill said: 'I know what he was like. After

Peggy died, I should have got you out of there.' That Bill had not seen me as the vile agent was valuable news.

Eventually, I told him that I'd known from day one how my mother had died. He was incredulous. I insisted that I'd been much better off knowing, and that I'd always be grateful to Derek. Not only did he seem to understand. He offered to look out some of my mother's belongings; he still had one or two, he thought. I said I'd be grateful, not letting on how much I coveted any small thing which might usefully jog my memory. I wrote him a long, brotherly letter, but he didn't reply. I wrote again; nothing. I'd mishandled it, probably; been too needy. I didn't bother him further.

I had one other possible witness – Derek's Aunt Daw in Brighton. With Dorothy Wickham – the only person in the world who's allowed to call me Pete – you simply don't beat about the bush. I told her I was in trouble, and asked if she had anything she could tell me. Immediately, she became furious about my grandfather: 'Got to you, too, did he? When your mum died, I let him have it: "*You* did that. You *killed* her, good as. Satisfied now, are you?"'

What had she meant? 'Oh, he bullied you but he'd done exactly the same to your mum and uncles. When we were all kids together, remember, we lived next door and we heard most of what was going on, saw a lot, too. *At* them all the time, he was, bawling, raging, for *nothing*. Your Uncle Bill got out of it, Jack cleared off, but Peggy, she couldn't escape.

'*He* drove her to it. I bloody told him. I never spoke to him again, either.'

The idea that Pop's bullying had been a major cause of my mother's death was appealing in so far as it reduced my own portion of guilt. That Daw had stuck it to him, too, gave me a passing rush of *schadenfreude*. But I could no more accept that he'd been entirely responsible for my mother's death than I could accept my grandparents' identical thesis about my father.

Of all Daw was able to tell me, the most valuable thing was that

Pop had bullied all his children, not only me. I hadn't known that. But as Daw had explained: 'He bullied the life out of all of you, Pete. It was just your turn.'

I don't believe that depression is a sign of moral failure, but it's humiliating to live what feels like half a life, and I do sincerely wish I could *buck up*. As disgusting as they are, however, depressions are not for nothing: there's stuff at the bottom of the pit.

A while after talking with Bill and Daw, for example, I felt freer to address the long-stuck matter of my mother and me. I didn't need telling that suicide is the worst pain anyone can inflict upon another. But I had always felt sorrier for my mother than I had for myself . . . What a trick! Such a simple means of denial. Now accepting it as such, I seemed to break through not into sorrow – been there, done that – but into the most enduring consequence of her suicide: the sense it left me of my own worthlessness.

Thirty years on, it even had an occasional physical manifestation. I'd be walking in the street when the pavement would suddenly seem to tip and I'd be *gone*, confidence shot, and barely able to keep my balance. A few steps of 'practice' walking – self-consciously keeping my hips square and carefully placing one foot in front of the other – and I'd be all right again. Then I remembered: when it had first happened, a couple of months or so after my mother's death, I'd fallen over, blitzed, as if I'd just heard the dreadful news.

Here was the nub of something: I still felt greatly loved by my mother, and yet I was for ever being harried and cornered by this sense of worthlessness. More than a paradox, it seemed to be the core script of my manic depression: absurdly high and delighted (much-loved 'sunshine' mode), crashed back into the pit ('worthless' mode).

Lots of other things now seemed explicable. Starting back with Victor and Halina, I never could quite understand what there was about me that they could like. As glad as I was of their affection, it always puzzled me – as with every lover and friend since.

The depressions still come and go like enforced winters. Sometimes they leave me empty-handed, sometimes not. I made a good find about a year ago. Since my early teens, I'd had a very occasional nightmare so terrifying that it would cauterise the memory: I'd remember I'd had it before only when I had it again; a day later it would be gone, until the next time.

The plainclothes policeman and I go back a long way. He knows me as well as I know myself, and is always friendly. Yet he is also anonymous; I can never make out his face. Aside from me, only he knows for certain that I committed murder, and he's just dropped by again to tell me he's within an ace of locating the final proof. That's the whole dream.

The terror was never about the prospect of being found guilty or punished. It was knowing with such certainty that I had committed murder that the conviction would stay with me for some hours after waking. Not bang-bang television murder; the sure knowledge that I had taken a life. To borrow from Conrad: *the horror*.

This time, though, I remembered to remember the dream, wrote it down, and made a point of telling it to a couple of friends. If I could register it, fix it in consciousness, perhaps I could undo its power.

Less than a week later I had a brand new dream. Three eyewitnesses have come forward to testify that I had killed no one; they're waiting to meet me at a solicitor's office. Some nasty people, who don't want this to happen, are after me but I manage to escape downhill on a monocycle with a peculiar wheel – an old-fashioned, two-colour type-writer rubber with a chromium hub, the kind my mother used. My dream character is extremely excited because he knows (as I do in waking life) that, since my mother died, I have never once dreamed of her, nor of any recognisable allusion to her. But now this, her typing rubber: the means of my escape, and a tool of erasure.

Cut to: Downtown, outside the solicitor's building. There's a woman with her arm through mine. I know who she is but, after so long, I don't dare look. Just before we enter, I look across at another building, and recognise the window of our toast-scented bedsit; above, two tall chimneys turn against the sky. Everything is so literal and accurate – right place, right company, a wholly sensible order of business.

Cut to: Interior of solicitor's office. Three men stand in front of his desk – my grandfather, badly injured and covered with blood; my Uncle Bill, curved over, exhausted; the third man is too short to be my father or me – oh, yes, it's my Uncle Jack, looking pale.

Plain to see that it had cost my three witnesses a lot to get here. The solicitor has already taken down sheaves of their absolving testimony. I turn to look at my mother, who squeezes my arm and smiles. Christ, how I love the round of her cheek, the set of her shoulder. The zinging texture of closeness is inimitably hers and mine. The only thing 'wrong' is actually right: she's looking up at me. For over thirty-five years, I've been taller than she was.

Dream as wish fulfilment? Not at all: the plainclothes policeman won't be back with his accusation of murder. The horror has evaporated, and I know now who the policeman was. I never did make out his face but his clothes were always familiar: they were mine; he was me.

For all their brittle euphoria, the up phases of manic depression are so welcome that they can con you into believing you've been into the pit for the last time. Experience teaches you to be more careful. This is good, you tell yourself, but take it easy, keep it level. Then the descent begins again. Therapy helped me to cope better, and I don't envisage being brought to my knees again, but anti-depressant drugs don't work for me. They make the pit foggier, is all. I can't time-travel back and undo my mother's suicide or prevent myself being blitzed by it. I had no resistance then, and have little even now. My much-loved 'sunshine' self was real; so was my worthless self. My edge against despair is the hope of undoing this mess.

As to the matter of my mother's suicide, it's as if I've begun to address it only recently. I've tried to come at it before, to push it, and with good reason. As I know from looking to dreams for useful information, you can bring a consumerly approach to the mind, and you will get a good return, for a while. Then, nothing. Whatever it is that's got a hold on you, it switches, as if from a loosened hammerlock to a rigid headlock, and you have to begin your moves all over again.

You can't out-think the heart; it doesn't recognise thought; the intellect is a thing of glue and matches. You can't trick the heart, either; it knows more than you do. The one thing it doesn't know about is linear time. Yesterday, forty years ago, it's all the same. My dumb lump doesn't even know how old I've become.

As far as I've got with the matter of my mother's suicide, I don't blame her. I'm familiar enough with depression to know she had no other way of stopping the unendurable. I'm far more fortunate. I can name the trouble I'm in, I have friends at the pit surface looking out for me. My mother was long gone from other people and any possible help. I take her suicide personally – bloody right, I do. I am fantastically angry. I am not worthless. The foolish thing is, I know she meant me no harm.

VALERIE GROVE

Laughter in Paradise

Nobody had a father like mine. Nobody else's father was so smiling and easygoing, friendly and funny. My pa was a cartoonist, which set him apart from other fathers from the start. In the road where we lived in my childhood in South Shields, everybody else's father went away to sea: they were Captain This or That. My pa too had been to sea, but he came home in the year I was born and, at thirty, fulfilled his life's ambition. He was taken on by the local paper, the *Shields Gazette* ('Found wherever a British ship sails,' proclaimed the masthead) to do a nightly strip about a naval cadet called Brassie. A woman up the road named Mrs Carter memorably said, 'Is that all?' when told what he did for a living. Cartooning looks too much like fun to be work – and it is true. Cartooning came as naturally to Pa as breathing. He never sat in a theatre or school hall without doodling faces all over the programme. His 'Smile with Smith' cartoon appeared for ten years on the front page of the *Evening Chronicle* in Newcastle, so he was a household name locally, but his ambition was to make it to Fleet Street. When I was fourteen he achieved it, so we moved to London. But I went back there at eighteen, in what was not then called my gap year, to learn journalism on the *Shields Gazette*; and when I turned up on doorsteps with notebook in hand, it was: 'You're Doug Smith's daughter? Come in.'

I was so proud of him. Other people's fathers were absent, strict, silent, distant, wrapped in their own concerns, boring. My daddy was there, always cheerful; he would join in, go swimming, walk the dog to the beach, play tennis, make posters when we put on plays, drive us to the riding school. Later, unlike other men obsessed by their cars, he let us drive his car to school while he took the tube. He never said no to anything we asked. My memory is of him fishing for fistfuls of coins in his pocket. He would come to the school to give one of his talks, performing his lightning cartoons on a huge easel covered in sheets of paper, and only laughed when my thicko London schoolfellows mocked his dear Geordie accent.

He was only fifty-six when he died, an age which seems increasingly youthful to me as I proceed with dismaying speed through my forties. It makes me brutal about other people's parents dying in old age. Died at eighty-seven, eh, well, well. What do they expect? The lead news item today as I write is about a woman of eighty-nine who had a heart attack and died in a hospital after waiting four hours to see a doctor; national scandal, immediate enquiry, terrible indictment of NHS, etc. Well, sad it is, for her family. But death, like birth, is a dreadfully personal matter. There can be no shock like being told that your adored father, active, sporting fit, never ill in his life, is in hospital having had a heart attack at forty-nine. I will never forget that journey to King's Cross from Newcastle not knowing whether I would see him alive again, when I was eighteen.

Pa had been cartooning since childhood. He was the middle one of three boys; in the family snaps he looks like Just William. He and his elder brother Allison in their childhood ran a family newspaper called the *Onlooker*. Allison wrote it and Pa illustrated it; Allison became a journalist, but died tragically young of asthma at twenty-nine. It seemed to me that Pa's family, what was left of it, consisted mainly of aged spinster aunts, like Bertie Wooster's. They made visitations upon us, pressing half-crowns into one's infant palm. Aunts Ella and May ran a tea-shop in South Shields, selling penny loaves, Aunt Ella being a source of great fascination since she had been dropped as a baby and her head lay permanently on one side. Toothless, witch-like Great Aunt Dora in black bombazine once took us to Tynemouth beach and said 'I've packed some biscuits, for fear we feel faint', which became a family catchphrase. Aunt Ina's tiny husband, Great-Uncle Laurie once commented that the lettering in the *Onlooker* seemed to have 'looked upon the wine when it was red'. This Bible-quoting, puritanical strain in the family was definitely not passed on to my father, who said he 'would not cross the street to go into a church'. But whenever there was a family wedding he would get on famously with the officiating clergyman of whatever persuasion, especially with bibulous Catholic priests.

He had been around the world twice over and the sepia snaps show him slim and handsome in uniform, in exotic harbours. I wish I'd written down his stories of life at sea on a tramp steamer which, he used to tell his audiences, was 'one step up from the gutter'. On his first trip to some foreign port – was it Marseilles, Rio de Janeiro, Shanghai? – a shipmate went ashore in a brand new cap he'd borrowed from Pa, got into a fight and was killed. His coffin was borne past his fellow ratings, with the cap placed on top. Pa said how close he had come to snatching back his new cap – how was he going to tell his mother?

Of course I loved him; he was so lovable. And he so obviously loved me. More important than loving, I liked him too. The playwright Dodie Smith, writing about her mother, says: 'True liking implies a reasoned judgement, and I have come to believe it is more important than loving: it wears better.' Long after her mother's death, she said she had no emotional sense of loss but 'I still find myself wishing to share things with her.' I could not put it better. It exactly sums up the kind of missing I still feel. Not a need to confide emotional things (although I could) but a longing to show him jokes and tell him stories that would make him laugh. There is no shared enjoyment in the world like shared amusement – watching someone's face erupt into the spontaneous Ha ha! as his always did. When I see cartoons, in *Private Eye* – he brought home for me the very first *Private Eyes*, which I still have – or the *New Yorker*, I want to show them to him, even today.

Each Friday he would take out a pile of library books and together we would race through them. The authors he introduced me to made jokes part of reading: Thurber, Wodehouse, S.J. Perelman, Damon Runyon. If I liked an author he disliked, like Ivy Compton Burnett, he was mystified. Pretentiousness baffled him. He revered Kipling, and Tennyson's *Idylls of the King*, and T.H. White's *The Once and Future King*, and E.B. White. Much of his literary pleasure came from America: the world of the *New Yorker*, the *Saturday Evening Post*, Raymond Chandler, Arthur Miller, Ed McBain, American cartoons: Pogo, Li'l Abner, Peanuts . . . He would chortle, then thrust the book in front of me, reading the passage aloud at top speed, the words obscured by the laughter. If you were reading and gave a quiet chuckle, 'At what do you tee-hee?' he would ask. Jokes had to be shared.

Nobody read as much as he did, or as chronically. He read while walking along the long road home from the tube, far too impatient just to walk. At home, he never sat in an armchair to read or do the crossword. He would kneel on the floor with the book or paper on the sofa. In the garden even on the dullest days, he would lie prone, buried in his book, his torso bare so his back was permanently brown. (I started to write this memoir in Spain, surrounded by low scrubby hills and in intense heat that he would have loved: olive-skinned and brown-eyed, like a native of the Mediterranean, he watched every day for any sign of the sun: 'I think it's trying to break through.')

Shakespeare was never daunting or boring, because Pa

familiarised me with characters and quotes that he relished – 'Let me have men about me that are fat'; 'She should have died hereafter'; 'the antic sits'. Though he left school at fifteen, he had read all the histories and tragedies on board ship, and loved *Richard III* with a particular passion, in spite of being entirely won over to Josephine Tey's argument in *The Daughter of Time*, and in the play *Young Dickon*, and the Paul Murray Kendall biography of Richard. Going with Pa to the Mermaid to see Paul Daneman as Richard was one of my dearest memories; years later I got to know Paul Daneman, and our friendship was entirely wrapped up in memories of Pa, and *Richard III*. One day Pa discovered that *Henry IV Part I* was being performed at the George in Southwark, and off we went together. Having Pa to do things with on Saturdays was my great daughterly privilege: watching soccer matches, playing tennis, getting books out, going swimming, going to films. How many times did we see *High Noon* (his favourite), *Gunfight at the OK Corral*, *The Magnificent Seven*, *Butch Cassidy and the Sundance Kid* – he knew everything there was to know about the frontier days of the Old West – and the movie of *Li'l Abner*, *Some Like It Hot*, *The Lost Weekend*, and *The Manchurian Candidate*? Today when I've seen a film he'd like I ache to tell him about it, and to see it a second time, enjoying his enjoyment.

He was so proud of me. 'My daughter's going to Cambridge.' He told everybody, at the slightest opportunity. ('Oh, Pa!' I would say; but didn't really mind.) Getting to Cambridge was something I wanted for him and for my English master. That was another lucky thing in my life: Mr Smart, an English master with a look in his eye that actually reminded me of my father's. What they each wanted for me turned out to be the same thing, and I wanted to please them both. So I worked hard, and the pleasure they both got from that telegram in December 1964 – AWARDED EXHIBITION GIRTON COLLEGE CAMBRIDGE – made that episode in my life hard to beat, ever, since they both had their faith in me vindicated and justified.

On the night he died, he was taken suddenly to Harefield Hospital, with a stroke. We were called to the hospital at 2 a.m. We waited for news, for about an hour. I misunderstood when the sister came in and told us there was no point in staying any longer, we could go home now; I was prepared to sit in hope for ever. I said, pathetically, 'Will you let us know then, if he dies?' She said gently, 'He died at three o'clock.' So that was it; it was over. As my mother and sister and I walked, crushed, to the car, my mother said, 'He was a nice daddy, wasn't he?' which was the sweetest thing she ever said.

He had come to see me that day, at my office at the *Evening Standard*, but I wasn't there. Damnably, I had been out reviewing the appalling film, *Jesus Christ Superstar*. A colleague who knew him told me next morning – I had to go in and write my reviews through eyes swimming in tears – how well he had looked. Pa had called in on the way to his own office, across Fleet Street, to tell them he would be coming back soon, after his heart bypass operation. Perhaps that was wishful thinking, perhaps he had a terrible presentiment, and needed to see me . . . well, I shall never know. I wasn't there.

Blake Morrison, in his book *When Did You Last See Your Father?*, describes travelling to see his terminally ill father and looking around the train at the 'deadbeat young Friday crowd with glazed eyes and Walkmans' and feeling, 'I'd have cheerfully swapped the life of anyone there for my father's.' I remember for a while resenting old men who were still alive, so many of them humourless, pompous, disgusting, smug. Why them? Why were they allowed to live, when they gave no pleasure? Why him? An obvious and banal reaction perhaps. But it lent me a fierce lack of sympathy, which remained as a sliver of ice in the heart.

The positive thing in my mourning him is that my guilt (about not seeing him that day, not seeing more of him in the previous weeks, not realising he might die, not saying goodbye) and my anger (about losing him) were short-lived. I 'got over it' astonishingly quickly; I had always said that my father's death would be the worst thing I could contemplate, yet I survived – well, I was twenty-seven and in charge of my life – and I actually thrived. Why? Because all my thoughts of him were loving. Of nobody else in the world could I say, categorically: he never annoyed me, and I don't think I annoyed him. He never, even now, reproaches me in spirit. I always wanted to see him, looked forward to seeing him, and enjoyed his company, and he knew that.

Pa influenced me totally, without even trying. He never said what he would like me to do with my life, but from infancy I wanted to go into journalism anyway, and it was plain that nothing would thrill him more. He wanted to work on the *Evening Standard* himself (a fool of an editor had turned him down when he was forty) so the fact that I went straight there from Cambridge was a sort of double fulfilment. My favourite babyhood photograph is of me at eighteen months on the floor of the *Shields Gazette* office, plonking a typewriter. Like a future politician outside Number 10, I thought my fate was sealed by that snapshot. But Pa never once used familiar parental clichés. He never said, 'When I was your age . . .' There were no reproaches for costing him money, no put-downs, no discouragements. He never made me feel small, unworthy, or belittled, or 'just a female', or less important than him.

When I needed help with anything he would give it – writing a puppet play when I was six, writing a debate speech in the sixth form. When I had to fill my own page for *Varsity* he did cartoons for it, to order. I was so lucky, so blessed. It truly astonished me when I first encountered fathers who routinely put down their daughters. The sort who said, 'Why do you want a career? You'll only get married.' I once watched my friend Alison's father counting the shillings in his purse, complaining how much her university fees would cost him: how loathsome, how baffling. I gradually came to realise that most women regarded their mothers as their great allies, their fathers as bugaboos. The psychiatrist author of *Fathers and Daughters* – one of several books that have been written on the subject – was astonished to discover how many unconfident women who came to him for therapy failed to identify their fathers as the source of their troubles with men and with life in general. But I could see that for most girls their mothers were the supporters, their fathers inspired anxiety. In our family those roles were reversed. It was Pa who never raised his voice to us.

He called us 'Chicken Licken' or 'Lovey'. I was Three-D (threepence) and my sister Two-D (tuppence). I'm glad the two of us accompanied him on his last holiday – a hilarious jaunt with the Cartoonists' Club to the ghastly-sounding Hotel Pontinental in Torremolinos. No pa loved having two daughters more. If anyone ever asked if he'd wanted a son, he'd say, 'After ten years on a ship with nothing but men I'd have been happy never to see another man for life.' Most memorably when at fourteen I fell in love one night with a beautiful young man who had but one arm ('and the popular prejudice,' as Pa's younger brother Cecil used to say, adapting Dickens on one-eyed Squeers, 'runs in favour of two') Pa thought of a good joke about it at once: 'What are you going to buy him for Christmas – a glove?'

I adored his friends. They were so funny. They were mostly in newspapers and seemed glamorous and witty and fond of racontage. Storytelling was all, and they told them so well. 'Wot cheor, me boy?' Pa would greet them, the Geordie hello. The first three journalists I met, between the ages of six and fourteen, were all his friends on the *Newcastle Chronicle*: Angus McGill, later of the *Evening Standard* and still my great friend; Harold Williamson, later with *Man Alive* on BBC-2, famous as 'the man who talks to children'; and the late Tom Bergman, Czech-born film critic who later became the companion of Mrs Gerard Hoffnung. Through them I knew that newspapers equal fun and laughter.

My mother detested Fleet Street and mistrusted journalists –

boozy boorish men and loud flirtatious women. She did not make friends with strangers as he did, or make allowances for people, as he did, keeping friendships alive for life. They inhabited different worlds.

The week after he died, I was interviewing Sir Osbert Lancaster about his London childhood. I walked numbly round Notting Hill with him, feeling treacherous to be buttering up this most senior cartoonist who was, for all his brilliance as creator of Maudie Littlehampton, not a jot as jolly or as agreeable as my pa. Pa got on with everyone; he could not be bored or aloof. But then Sir Osbert had reached the pinnacle of cartoon fame, and Pa had not. To the end of his life Pa was still trekking off to godforsaken places to give his talk – it was called 'Quick on the Draw,' and went down splendidly with audiences across the USA as well as at home – for small sums like six guineas, to libraries and luncheon clubs and Boy Scouts and Rotaries and Over-60s. Always the same cartoons – the desert island joke, the cannibal joke, the football joke, the wartime joke, the domestic joke. It galled him that he never broke into television with it. And that although he was published in the *Saturday Evening Post,* his work was never accepted by *Punch*. Among the relics he left, I find *Punch*'s friendly rejection slips: 'Sorry Doug but these are "not quites" I'm afraid' – and I know how much this wounded him. When I started being asked to write for *Punch* he was pleased. The day of his funeral, *Punch* carried a picture of its summer trip to Boulogne: there was I with Alan Coren, William Davis, Barry Humphries, Bill Tidy. He'd have enjoyed seeing that but it was just too late.

Pa had a heart bypass three weeks before he died. After that operation he looked stricken, in the hospital bed which makes even the most dynamic person look pathetic. He was exasperated to be immobilised and dependent. And hated being 'among all these low-lifers', uncongenial dreary folk, a caged tiger. Never was a man less likely to be a patient patient. He would have been an impossible invalid if he'd lived on but had become incapacitated, unable to draw or to read.

I notice increasingly that all the things he liked become more and more important to me. For years, as lullabies to my children, I sang nothing but 'Don't Fence Me In', 'Stormy Weather', 'Do Not Forsake Me, Oh My Darling' and 'Ol' Man River', his favourite songs. And why have I suddenly started doing crosswords?

In twenty years, not a day has passed without thinking of him. He is in my head and heart. Although I physically resemble him and recognise what I inherited from his genes or from his nurturing – laughter, artistic ability, impatience – I wish I could be more truly like him in character, that I had his sweet nature. I wish I knew how you get a child to feel the total, trusting adoration he so artlessly made me feel for him. I wish he could have met my husband who is as nice as he, but I only fell in love with him a year after Pa's death. (I was incredulous to find myself so happy again, and so renewed. My first marriage had been falling apart that same summer that Pa died.) And I wish with all my heart that he could have known his grand-children. It is terrible to discover how family history repeats itself. His own father died at fifty-six too, before I was born; my mother used to tell me, 'Your grandfather was a kind, sweet man, he would have loved you, he would have taken you to the beach and bought you ice-creams.' And when my children were younger and asked me about my father, I found myself saying the same things: 'My daddy would have loved having grandchildren. He would have loved reading to you and doing little drawings for you . . .' Our children know so few old men because so few have survived. And although I feel that he is inside me, as I write, I am sad that it is impossible for my children ever really to know what he was like.

But I have loved writing about him. I feared it would make me cry, and it did. But mostly I feel only positive things, undying love and gratitude. I wish he could appear beside me right at this minute. He'd say, 'What's this, lovey?' looking over my shoulder. He'd laugh to read such stuff about himself, least vain of men. He'd say 'Ho yus!', which was his way of brushing something aside. It makes me happy though just to sit here thinking about him. He was the dearest man and I was the luckiest girl to be his daughter, his Chicken-Licken. No matter what happens, they can't take that away from me.

JEAN MCNEIL

November

The funeral home was a faithful imitation of a nineteenth-century Louisiana bordello. The wallpaper a thick textured red, the curtains a heavy velveteen, again a deep, even more vermilion red. All that was missing were the hard-faced adolescents trailing lace and brocaded underwear from room to room. I remembered reading somewhere that red made you hungry, and simultaneously felt my stomach rumble.

Charlie Francis, the funeral home director, stood by the door, clammily clasping hands as quickly as people had withdrawn them from their winter gloves.

'Cancer is gold to him,' I thought, thinking of the reason most corpses reached this room. His permanent expression of sympathy – the sagging lip, the hollow cheeks, the wide glassy eyes full of empathy – had a fish-like cast. Why are undertakers always men? That the job is too distasteful for women's sensibilities sounds a gracefully outmoded Victorian notion. Charlie's two sons were in the business as well, and they attended him like an imperial guard, clad in bad suits and flanking their father with their hands clasped behind their backs.

While pretending to inspect the condolence cards, which had been shoved into a contraption that I can only compare with a plastic church candle rung round with a slinky, I overheard two women. They were ancient relatives, I guessed, possibly cousins of my grandfather, and were speaking in sombre, confidential voices near the coffin.

'I never expected him to go the way he did,' the smaller woman, who had a crumpled, flat-tyre face, breathed.

Her companion was heartier, still flush-cheeked. 'No, that man was the best driver I've ever seen.'

'He took one chance too many. It's the law of averages.'

'He knew he wasn't going to die for a long time. Look how many times he almost went, and came back. He must have just been sick of it all.'

There were women who went to wakes just to utter this kind of melodramatic appraisal of the deceased's life and demise. In our community wakes were the equivalent of church socials: a chance to see your old friends, a chance to reminisce. And a chance to drink. At least one of those demure older women had a mickey in her purse.

I stepped up beside them.

'Oh, his granddaughter.' The crumpled-faced woman introduced me to the other woman.

'He was a fine man,' she said. 'You should be proud to have a grandfather like him.'

My mind goes numb in the face of platitudes, so I only managed to smile in response.

'Oh, you're so tall now,' the crumpled-faced woman cooed, breaking the silence. 'It's hard to believe how big you've grown. You're a real little lady now. Have you got a boyfriend?'

'No. Have you?'

Silence. They tried to smile, but couldn't.

I liked stopping conversations, and freezing smiles on people's faces.

'I gave commands. Then all smiles stopped together.'

I used to recite 'My Last Duchess' to him, from beginning to end. I wanted to be the Duke of Ferrara, and not the innocent Duchess.

He taught me to want that.

These are the coordinates: 47°N, 60°L. If you look at a map of Nova Scotia you will see the ungainly shape, like a too-large head on a frail body, or a question mark in reverse. It hardly looks like an island. One mile of water is all that separates it from the mainland. But that one mile width is also one mile deep: one of the deepest guts in the Atlantic. It is formed by a trough in the North American continental shelf, a seam so deep that even when they had blasted away half a mountain to build the causeway, they could not fill it.

I am the sixth generation to be born on the Island. I am the second generation to have left for good. The first was my mother, but she doesn't count. My grandfather left many times, often to travel far, but he always came back. He was a musician, and he played the fiddle, the electric guitar, the blues harmonica, the accordion, and the spoons. He sang unaccompanied, and while his voice was not sweet or accurate, the dry-throated passion with which he sang often moved his audience to tears.

My grandmother was a devout woman, a Catholic. She was good to me. She died a year and a week before my grandfather. I suspected he lasted just long enough to spite her – a year was a nice symmetrical measure of time – and then he'd had enough.

'I'm played out,' he said to me over the phone when he called me in Paris. Which meant, in our local dialect, exhausted.

November is coming around again. I treat the month with a mixture of fear and loathing bordering on the ferocious; I regard it as I would a mamba in the jungle, coiled to strike. It is the only month that chases me around the calendar, the only one I can *feel* the whole year, even in the midst of a July heatwave.

I have friends who say things like: 'I'm not afraid of death for myself, but for my children' or, 'I know that it doesn't stop at death, it just can't.' My reaction is always one of seething silence at these mellifluous statements, uttered by people who look wide-eyed and bewildered, like lambs about to be led to the slaughter.

I am unequivocal about my fear of death, and the unapologetic anger I feel that anyone has to die at all. I have no questions to ask on that subject. I have been to my fair share of funerals, considering my age.

Why do I mourn him more? It should have been her. She was the one who saved me, who saved me from him. This feeling is what the churchmen must mean when they pull out that scalloped and gilded word from their sermon repertoire. Guilt.

Ever since I could remember, my grandfather had been trying to die, and not succeeding. For me this meant another night spent in another ditch on the side of the highway, the stars and moon slaughtering the northern sky above our dazed heads.

'Grandpa, are you OK?'

Bright, carmine blood dripped from my grandfather's nose on to the steering wheel. He sniffed.

'Jesus,' he swore, which meant yes.

Slowly, we extricated ourselves from the car. I climbed out through the half-open window, as my door was jammed against the incline of the bank. My grandfather walked right out, shutting the door carefully behind him. The night was cool, and I shivered, as I wore only a T-shirt and a thin pair of trousers. I looked around at the black hulks of the brooding pines, the unlit highway barely visible, trying to calculate how many miles' walk we had until we reached home.

'Think I'll flag someone down,' my grandfather muttered while wiping his bloody nose on his sleeve.

'You know people stop quicker if I do it,' I reminded him, stomping up the bank to stand on the gravel shoulder. I knew that the sign of a young girl next to an accident site in the dead of the night scared people into stopping – more out of sentimentality than concern, probably: a child in danger! a potential orphan! I already sensed that most people were suckers as far as children went. As they braked from sixty or seventy miles an hour their tyres wrote crazy messages of haste and foreboding on the road.

But Grandpa was never dead. He usually sat on a stone on the side of the ditch, holding his head, looking and feeling sorry for himself.

'Is he all right?' the solicitous man or woman would ask me.

I would shrug my shoulders.

'He's drunk.'

After the funeral I drove back to the house and walked into the kitchen, where everyone had gathered for tea and sandwiches. Within the busy, convivial atmosphere people were catching up with one another. Two cousins – both young women – had joined the army. This was the only way they could get their university tuition paid. Jane had tried to fund her law school education by working in the bank. In the end she joined the air force. Connie, who was training to radar monitor, really wanted to be a fashion designer.

'These kids are barely twenty and are getting 18,000 dollars a year,' Connie's father said appreciatively. 'And they get an education.' I was about to argue about the ethics of being human ammunition toys for the state when he spoke again.

'They wouldn't take me because of my arm.' He looked down to where the artificial limb, a result of a close encounter with a cement mixer when he was sixteen, poked out of his sleeve.

Everywhere people were smiling, people were pressing food into my hand. It was carnivalesque, a kind of northern reprise on the Day of the Dead celebrations. Everything seemed to come at me from a long way away, as if I were looking out of the wrong end of binoculars. I noticed that most of my relatives were drinking. I wondered how soon I could get a plane out.

'Jean-Marie,' my Great-Aunt Mary approached me, using the name I had renounced many years ago as too hillbilly for my sensibilities. 'I know you'll be lonely, but he's happy now. You mustn't feel sorry for yourself.' She put an arm around my shoulders, but drew it away when I flinched involuntarily.

Behind me, like the chorus in a Greek tragedy, I knew what the women were whispering.

'Poor Thing, No Mother and No Father.'

'What happened?'

'The father was never around. Never heard tell of him.'

'And the mother?'

'The mother disappeared in Africa. Tragic, tragic.'

And the women's voices warbled down to a thin gruel-like sound.

'May God accept his soul into his kingdom,' Aunt Mary said piously, still standing next to me, hoping for an appropriate response, so that she could leave me with a clear conscience and go and get another sandwich.

'We hew an image out of our fear and call it God,' I thought, remembering Squire Jons's line in *The Seventh Seal*. Behind me, the whispering women continued.

'She was so devoted to her grandfather.'

'And him such a bastard.'

'No he wasn't.'

'Yes he was.'

'No he wasn't . . .'

I had come home from Paris, where I was studying, for the funeral. The churchyard looked tiny and uninhabited to me, with its well-spaced two dozen or so graves, all neatly tended and most less than a hundred years old.

In Paris, as in any European city, death is related to living arrangements in a way that strikes me as sinister. Tiny old people living in tiny apartments which they have sold off before their death to a younger couple, who fantasise about the death of the older couple, waiting with salacious fervour for them to die, so that they can claim their new home. Or bribing the council for a minute grave plot, where you lie arse to shoulder like a tin of sardines, or being shunted to suburban cemeteries because you're not important enough to lie with the literati in Highgate Cemetery, or with the mournful corpses of *vedettes* who supposedly embody *la France* in Père Lachaise. Small lives, confined by the crush of many other bodies. Too many for the sagging, limpid landscape of a dying Europe to support.

Our lives, and his death, had been mauled by isolation. The question came walking down the road toward me; it had my face. It was like the doppelganger.

If he had been found earlier, would he have lived?

I have a very illogical mind, which, I am told by many eminent psychiatrists and self-help mythology, befits a woman. The illogicality of it manifests itself most spectacularly in my opinion that if we are to die, then I really don't see the point. What is the use of existing, if one day you are squashed as randomly as a fly trodden underfoot, and leave about as much as the residue and sum total of your physical existence? I believe in continuum, and immortality. I am not interested in flux or in disappearances.

This is what his death means to me: the death of all that rage, all that tortured aggression and self-pity. The energy that went into maintaining it, and the febrile mind which was the conductor of a sort of symphony of discontent. If he lived, then he lives. He can't have lived and then simply not live any more. What is this insane asylum we're locked into, the human body?

This is what I believed then, at the wake, staring at his heavily made-up body, which had to be straightened out beforehand on some kind of rack they kept in the basement of the funeral home.

I am told by the same psychology of bereavement books whose tone is an amalgam of the excruciatingly sympathetic and the didacticly brusque that we become more accepting of death as time goes on. I have never bought any of these books. They belong to a friend. I have browsed through them desultorily.

I am unapologetically angry and accept nothing that has to do with endings, or change. I can't finish books for fear of them ending. And I refuse to think of anyone, especially him, as dead. He is simply somewhere else.

The books tell me this is a common reaction.

His sisters had the firm-legged stance of experienced mourners. We stood in a semi-circle around his grave, holding hands. Tears coursed down their crumpled faces, and now that they were old I saw that they were the spitting image of my great-grandmother, their mother. I would not cry. As a matter of principle I do not take part in public displays of emotion. The silence of the afternoon was like a ball of dough in your hand: you could knead it, feel its malleable thickness. The blue mountains faced the graveyard, utterly wordless and worn down, being the last tracks of the Appalacians and older than the rest of the continent.

'Do you remember the time he brought the racoon into the house to keep for a pet?' his sister Mary had reminisced the night before, as we sat in a row on the chesterfield. 'My God, he could be sentimental about animals.'

'Do you remember the time the house caught fire and he ran back and forth from the brook with buckets of water?' his sister Alice said. 'I'll never forget the sight of him dousing the roof with his pathetic little dungarees flapping in the wind.'

My great-grandmother cooked in the lumber camps in the winter. From the age of twelve, my grandfather had been left to care for his sisters and his half-brother. In the spring, my great-grandmother would come back with a new boyfriend from the camps. I saw a picture of my grandfather at this age once. His face was not the face of a twelve-year-old.

Sitting beside his sisters on the couch the evening before the funeral, I felt they were talking about someone I had known only peripherally. And in a way, this was true. To him, he was not father, or grandfather, but Charlie. Someone who had been a child, someone who had cried and who had been afraid in the night. He had existed long before I ever had, and I realised that despite the abundance of black-and-white photos of his life this had never quite come home to me before.

He was more to them than he ever was to me. Because I had come too late, when he had already begun the long process of dying.

It was New Year's night. We could smell the fire on the wind. From the sea-facing window of our trailer we saw the black sky, scorched and toxic with the flames and smoke. Through the gusts of the blizzard wind, the flames rattled into sight, and then disappeared behind another white blanket of driven snow.

'That's a fire at the Brodies',' my grandfather said, and went to the bedroom to get his rifle. 'Get your snowsuit on,' he called behind him as he walked down the narrow corridor.

'You're not taking her,' my grandmother said flatly, as if she expected she would win.

'I Jesus well am,' snarled my grandfather. 'I need some company.'

We put our snowshoes on in front of the shed, although by then the snow had drifted around our ankles like incoming waves. I coaxed our dog out from her house. The border collie instantly smelled the fire, and the red sky leapt and shattered in her wide brown eyes. We headed off through the woods then, with only the flashlight and my grandfather's knowledge of his own land to guide us to the shore.

The blizzard blinded us. I only remember seeing the arc of light from my flashlight as I shone it on the tails of my grandfather's advancing snowshoes. Creatures, black as coal and with red rings in their eyes, entwined themselves with the close trees, and let us pass. Underneath the cap of the tall pines the roar of the wind and the sea was strangely distant, muffled by the dense moss and many eyes of startled animals. The dog bounded ahead when we came to the first clearing, and disappeared beneath the waves of snowdrifts only to bound out again in the next stride. She seemed to be built on springs as she got further and further ahead.

'She's got a good nose,' my grandfather yelled over his shoulder, and I caught his words just before they were swallowed by the wind.

Our snowshoes brushed silently through the snow, and our tracks were instantly covered behind by the wolf-howling winds that came to the island off the Atlantic. When we reached the woods we could see the orange light again through the trees. And when we came to the shore, where the cabin stood burning, glass shattered in one of the upstairs rooms. It left small trenches in the snow where it fell, like the icicles parachuting from the eaves on an early spring day.

I looked across at my grandfather's face as we stood on the edge of the moss and sand, uncertain in the face of the heat and the flying sparks. It too seemed to crack into shards of fear as he saw the fire. His thin brittle eyebrows bristled in the heat. He had been burnt when he was a tank driver in Sicily, but I didn't know that then. He hated confined spaces and he hated fire more. I only saw the apprehension scramble over his face like a crab, and then it was gone.

The dog barked and we saw that old Brodie was standing in the driveway barefoot in his white nightgown and cap, looking like Scrooge. He didn't seem to see the dog, and was looking beyond the light thrown by the flames to some indeterminate point in the forest.

'Go to him,' said my grandfather, and threw me one of the blankets he had carried down.

The forest cracked on the back of the blizzard wind, and shattered, as more of the upstairs windows blew out.

And then Grandpa disappeared into the red and black mess of the burning cabin.

The next morning the dog and I sat in the bathtub, which had landed in the driveway and was now full of snow. I made snowballs and the dog licked at the sides of the tub. Flurries were still floating down, but the storm had moved out to sea. My grandfather was picking through the blackened wreck that surrounded the chimney, the only part of the house that had been left standing.

'Got a saucer . . . got a doorknob!' he yelled to me, and held up the half-charred relic triumphantly, then stooped over again, trying to retrieve something of the old couple's lives.

The Brodies had slept in my grandparents' bed in the trailer until the ambulance arrived from Sydney Mines. Mrs Brodie had been singed a little as my grandfather had carried her out of the burning walls. Mr Brodie suffered from shock and mild hypothermia. Grandpa had dragged them both back to the trailer on my play sled. They were huddled in heavy blankets, and I had to push them from behind, my small hands on the Brodies' frail and trembling backs, my heels dug into the snow, as we went uphill back to the trailer. I thought I had heard old Brodie crying between gusts of wind.

Ahead of me, I watched my grandfather's stooped back, the sled rope taut around his chest, the rifle slung over his shoulder on its strap, his eyes on the dog who made our path back through the woods. He turned to me from time to time, to make sure that we were all right.

I trudged, my hands around the old couple's shoulders, thinking that I would follow my grandfather, as I followed him now through the storm, over our land, over our years on the island, for ever.

'Christie, you were my girl,' he had sobbed over my grandmother's coffin the year before. 'I never loved anybody but you.'

Those of us sitting around the coffin rolled our eyes and shook our heads. His girlfriend of the time sat a few feet away, behind his heaving shoulders.

We are not a stoic people – we leave that to our Presbyterian cousins. Given the opportunity, we will melodramatise situations. Drunk or not, it is inevitable. One of the ways this manifests itself is our penchant for making an icon out of the dead.

I began to fantasise about saving him, that I had been there, really. In my daydream, I was Max von Sydow in *The Seventh Seal*, and Death was my adversary.

On that night, I faced the chasm of the four-lane Trans-Canada Highway and, across the four lanes of death, I saw him on the other side. The same wind that whipped my hair flapped the black sails of his robes against the tall masts of his legs. I could see that he was made for fighting this weather: he could see in between the cold plodding snowflakes, his eyes did not water from the iceberg wind.

I stood on the shoulder of the westbound traffic, with transport trucks hurtling through the thin November evening, their orange lights illuminating the sky, shaking the earth as they slipstreamed past.

Death stood on the other shoulder, right by that area of embankment that had cost so many drivers their lives. He looked just like I had imagined him: a feral animal crossed with whatever po-faced Swede had played Death in Bergman's film.

Death's face was not visible, but I could tell that he was leering at me all the same. And then the skies broke forth with the sounds of Carl Orff's *Carmina Burana*, the long low rumbling of the tenors and the dim, quick chanting of the sopranos: 'Christi, Christi, Christi', the cold medieval voices coming across dread-inspired centuries of time, from their suspicious, carnivorous landscape of squalor and austere religious fervour. The sopranos broke through with their voices crying for me to beat him, to make him know once and for all that Death was finished, outmoded and dim-witted, and that I was standing on that stretch of the Trans-Canada Highway so that I could fight him, beat him, so that I could win.

The night before the funeral, as we all sat together in his girlfriend's house, drinking, it suddenly occurred to me to ask where the rum we were drinking came from.

'The bottle in the car,' said Mary.

'Which car?' I asked.

'His. Can't let a nearly full bottle of Navy Rum go to waste.'

I ran to the door and hurled the glass out into the night, where I heard it shatter in the distance. His dog whimpered.

When I came back, I said, 'That's what killed him. We are drinking his blood.'

His sisters looked at me blank-eyed. They could see I had inherited one thing for sure: I was a Drama Queen.

Mother and Father. What do these words mean? In the biblical sense, the meaning is carnal. They had more than a hand in your making. By my definition, they are the people who care for you. They might be the wolves and bears of fairy tales, raising feral lost children. They might be millionaire film stars who can't conceive, and so adopt a child from a disadvantaged part of the world. One thing is for certain, and Shakespeare backs me up on this: they are roles, they are ideals. An abstract concept, as strange as the thought of Eve springing from Adam's rib.

I never worried that they were older than other children's parents. They were still young, relatively speaking, when they inherited me. They had time and room to love me, even though my grandfather was becoming more erratic and violent through the effects of his alcoholism. My grandmother, who generally scorned knowledge and education, had taught me how to write and do sums before I went to school.

I think of myself as a bridge truncated. They died before I had time to take the full measure of the gut they spanned, the dangerous, swirling water over which they held me aloft.

'Where do you stop and where do I begin?' I might have asked them, but they wouldn't have told me the answer. Is this the question children ask their parents, who had an actual biological hand in their creation? Are the boundaries more blurred, or delicately delineated?

Maybe I wouldn't know, even had they been my parents and I forty-two instead of twenty-two when he died. Even had I been old enough to know myself, and could measure the silences their deaths would cause to resonate throughout the rest of my life.

When did it occur to me that they would die? My grandmother had had cancer and lived to conquer the 'black bitch', as I called the disease, aping my grandfather's penchant for verbal histrionics. And I was convinced my grandfather was heroically indestructible. Others thought him a puerile, silly drunk. Manipulative, mean, violent, selfish, power-mad, and finally, after my grandmother and I left him in the middle of the night, truly mad. I considered it a sign of integrity in him to have gone mad.

My grandmother was far too sane to ever go mad. And she lacked the energy required.

'Pride is a sin,' she told me. You had to have pride to go mad. It was a tradition in our family for women to be martyrs, rather than mad people; circumstance didn't help, but there was a genuine trend for women to sacrifice themselves *ad infinitum*. I thought martyrdom provided a vocation in a culture where women did not normally hold jobs. I would have rather been a drunk than a martyr, hence I sided with my grandfather.

It was generally thought within the family that I sided with him because I knew that's where the power lay. The women couldn't believe that I would be so dim as to actually love him. There was a precise delineation in our culture, and in our family, as to where your allegiances should lie. Women depended on other women. And in our theatrical repertoire the women's roles were very limited: they were either The Beaten or The Fucked (or both). So for a granddaughter to side with her grandfather was an act of treason that could only be explained by the granddaughter's rampant sentimentalism and lack of good judgement.

The women knew I would get the money (what little of it there was). And I got the car. Or what was left of it, a crumpled mess, the roof caved in like a sunken soufflé. The car insurance, yes, I got that. I saw it enter my bank account.

At the wake, the women's voices whispered, 'Blood money.'

At the funeral I played two of my grandfather's favourite tunes, 'Farewell to Oban' and 'Hector the Hero'. There are few things so satisfying as playing music in tribute to someone you love. Then I sat down and listened to the rest of the Mass.

In his address the priest quoted a phrase of a psalm my grandfather had wanted read at his funeral. The words still sear me with their appropriateness:

'Such things were too wonderful for me, too high . . .'

I know the lines along which Grandpa had been thinking when he read this. He meant words were too wonderful, as opposed to music, which was the total expression of my grandfather's soul. And life, in a way, which was too wonderful for him. He could not make good, it seemed, out of life. He could never quite rise to the challenge of living for someone other than himself. Unlike the women, he never aspired to sainthood or martyrdom, but then he'd never been initiated at an early age into the cult of the Virgin Mary the way girls had been.

'Are you coming back to the house for sandwiches?' my Aunt Mary asked me after the funeral.

She, like everyone else, was treating me carefully, like a visiting foreigner whose habits were unpredictable.

'You go ahead. I'll come along in a few minutes,' I said, still clutching my fiddle. After everyone had gone and I was alone with the heap of dirt and the fake grass covering used to distract people from what it really was — the burial mound — I sat down on the steps of the church, and squinted against the yellow November light, which had become thick, suffused with a rich amber glow in the sunset.

My instinct is to put myself outside of gatherings and situations.

My impulse is to be alone. So I decided to drive the eight miles down the road to where it had all happened, where we had lived.

They were not in the graveyard, after all. They had gone home, so I would go there, too.

Many people lay claims to minor clairvoyance, which is usually a desire, in retrospect, not to admit that momentous happenings could come as a surprise. When the telephone had rung the week before, I knew. It rang differently. The sound was malevolent. I was reading a book of poems at the time, *Skin and Bones*, by Paula Gunn Allen. I put the book gently on the table and took a long time to walk to the phone. As I expected, it was my aunt's taut voice that entered my ear.

I knew already, before I heard that he was dead, that they were the sum total of all my parts. They had my past in their hands. They were the only ones who had known where I had come from: my mother, they had even met my father, whom I had certainly never had the dubious pleasure of encountering. And as long as one of them was alive, they were both alive, and I could see my life clearly, refracted in two prisms.

I think I howled. People came running.

When he died, I was finally free – of the past, or so I thought. What I didn't realise then was that only when completely bound are we completely free.

The west wind on the lake, the black sky. Why do the scrub-grass and the spidery alders turn rust red in November? As if the colours of the land announced, like a prophecy, the coming of the month of blood and the thin, old remnants of a past life. I look up into the sky and I see power sucked backwards by wind tunnels formed in between the shards of clouds, which are advancing, relentlessly, toward the sea. This is a wonderfully deranged, savage landscape, the ground breeding a shrill euphoria, like the passion of gospel singers wailing up into the rafters of a church. Crags, fjords, the earth breaking away in cracks and fissures as it falls into the sea.

I stand on the spot where our trailer stood, where it all happened. The sky is streaked alternately by green and purple. The birches gleam their pastel hue, the white bark reflecting the shifting colours of twilight. And around their band of luminescence the sky turns from deep blue to night.

It is November, almost winter. This is the dying time of year. Nothing of them remains; they are already turning to worm-sodden mud in their coffins. My grandmother has been in the ground a year and a week. She will have been nearly picked clean, the red silk blouse in which she was buried rotted to threads.

My grandfather has been in the ground an hour. I still want to pluck him out, dust him off, tell him that this is all some terrible mistake.

I drive down to the other house, the one that was first home. There is only a water tank to mark the place where the Big House stood. It is still green with the coat of paint my grandfather gave it the last summer we lived there. But around the edges rust is growing like a disease. The base of the chimney pokes out of the grass, where charred pieces of carbonised wood are still visible. The old foundations of the house have been swallowed up by the grass and the alder trees. Snakes course through the waves of long grass.

Like Shelley's Ozymandias, I am surrounded by the gutted monuments of self-proclamation: the foundations of a house once grand, and the flattened ground upon which the modest trailer stood; that few square feet where so much happened and is happening again, over and over.

I am a traveller in my own past; so I must be detached. I will not, for instance, see my grandfather, suddenly, spring up from the steep path that leads down to the brook, a bunch of wild roses in his hand, although the roses are long since withered on their stalks.

'Here,' he says. 'Throw these on my grave. It's a nice melodramatic gesture. I'm not in it anyway. I'm here. This is my home, as it was yours too.'

And the sun shines in June, and the strawberries grow ripe in the garden while the plums plummet from the thick branches of the tree beside the roses.

'Here,' he says, reaching for his hankie. 'Don't be all nostalgic.'

And this moment, with his emergence over the sharp crest of the hill to the brook (whose path has been hopelessly overgrown; I would have to stumble down to the spot where I used to watch the tadpoles squirming), this moment with the still black-haired man who holds roses in his hand, who ignores the sting of their thorns . . .

'Here,' he says. 'Take these for your grandmother. Tell her to find the biggest vase and put them on the kitchen table. It's my birthday today, and I'm going to make her happy.'

Happ . . . y . . . Happ . . . y . . .

The echo.

. . . that moment in the roses, by the brook, is happening for ever. It is happening now, revolving around me, as I stand here in this foreign city, as it happened on that November afternoon, with the scrub-brush tickling my ankles, with the car's headlights cutting through the thickening four o'clock gloom.

And the Big House rematerialises in front of me; its strong white wood is laid upon a scaffold of memories, the newly painted red shutters and the green tank, rustless and verdant, adorn the house. It is filled with the music of the musician's accordion, and the thud of dancing feet. It is stocked with china and with mahogany; it is full of toys and blankets and photographs of my lost mother, perfectly young, perfectly beautiful. Everything that happened in that house was at once lovely and sinister. And I shiver now, because I fear the animals are watching me from their hiding places on the edge of the woods. I fear the werewolf's sharp nail on my shoulder.

But my grandfather is coming toward me from the brook. He is wearing no shirt; it is a hot day in June, his birthday. He walked by the roses on the path, and their thorns have pierced his flesh. Small beads of blood glisten on the nicks scattered over his chest and his back.

'You look like Christ,' I laugh.

'I am Christ.' He is serious. And suddenly his neck is loose, his head hanging off his torso at an improbable angle. He is black and stiff. He has two days' stubble on his chin, two days' growth when his hair had continued to grow – when all other functions of his body had shut down – as he lay there, dangling upside down for thirty-six hours. The silent snow, choking all sound, the bloodless corpse. His harmonica, fallen out of his pocket, on the roof, which is now the floor. His cap, askew over his face.

So there won't be another night for him. Only this one when the stars are his ground and the ground his ceiling.

This was a man. He will never end for me. Both of them are revolving all around me, on that plane of timelessness that I believe runs parallel to our dim perception of time, and of life. I feel him more, I think, because I also couldn't seem to live up to anyone's expectations of what I should be. I was not, like my grandmother, a Good Woman. We were both on the outside, and I felt comfortable, there, with him. Now I had no company.

It is one of the first days of winter, and he is cold. He hangs upside down by straps. Waiting for that light to come arcing over the horizon from Greenland, the arctic promise of a new morning, the bare-boned timber trees, the thick harvest moon and the fields of autumn redberries. Waiting, for the music and the light, while the traffic passes above him.

And I understood him. There are very few people in your life you can ever hope to understand.

A man, a hot day in June, no shirt. A man, crucified by roses.

MARY SCOTT

In Her Own Right

My mother's funeral wasn't quite right. I don't mean that the flowers I'd chosen bloom by bloom in the florist's the day before were wilted and discoloured compared with the cellophane-wrapped off-the-peg efforts other people sent; although they were. I don't mean that the vicar who presided over the occasion was a stranger; although he was. I don't mean that the hymns weren't spot on; we'd selected them, like the flowers, with care. I don't mean that there was anything about the service *per se*; it was simple and short, just as we'd ordered. Nor was there anything in the brief epitaph spoken by my youngest uncle: anything to which you could take exception.

But he described someone I didn't know: a normal, ordinary, rather dull-sounding woman – his brother's wife – with a normal, ordinary family. And – another let-down – when some invisible mechanism beneath the coffin started up and carried her, to the accompaniment of soft Muzak, towards an apricot-coloured curtain and (presumably) to the flames beyond, no nameless Fury erupted either from within the coffin or in me.

I sat and wondered whether the whole body swiftly reduced to ashes or whether some bits – the bones, say – had to be incinerated longer. I wondered whether her platinum wedding ring which my father had insisted she take with her would melt; or would it be picked out later by a contemporary equivalent of a plunderer on a medieval battlefield? Of course it wouldn't. Crematorium workers would, like everyone else, have a Code of Practice. Besides, they probably never let the fire go out.

We trooped out of the chapel. Smoke billowed from a tall chimney, but I couldn't be sure it was hers.

To look at the smoke I had to screw my eyes against the sun. I'd always been the image of my mother; and now I didn't so much feel the expression on my own face as see its replica in front of me on hers. So did everyone else: the unfamiliar aunts, the distant cousins. They said so at the party afterwards, marvelled how meeting me was like being with Dorrie again after all these years. I even had her voice!

After the funeral my father handed me a fatly stuffed brown A4 envelope; it contained my mother's poems. The one on top was about me aged ten, dancing, pretending to be a pony. In the poem my mother foresaw my great future. The world would be my oyster; oysters would be mine for the asking. I would dance the night away, night after night, in a gorgeous gown, with a handsome chap in tow.

I'm ten. We're looking over a property with a view to making an offer. We always do that when we're on holiday.

We live (holidays apart) in a big, rambling house of which I'm very fond in a city which I hate: Middlesbrough. The house in the city has a stable and a loft above for hay. But you can't keep a pony in a city.

Look on the bright side, says my mother, we might live in the country one day – you never know how soon; and if we do, when we do, then, yes, you might have a pony.

The 'holiday' property – a whitewashed cottage – fronts on to a steep, car-clogged village street. At the back is an orchard, equally steep, with small, gnarled apple trees and a vicious tangle of brambly weeds. I stand on the edge of the jungle, too scared of scratches and of stings from nettles to explore. But a *pony* could push his way through: even a small, brown pony. When he did I wouldn't be wearing cotton shorts and an Aertex shirt. I would be wearing jodhpurs and a yellow, cable-knit, polo-necked jersey. I would be holding an apple from one of the trees on my outstretched hand; his lips would tickle my palm. Would I pat him next? I play the scene over and over, not sure what comes next.

We didn't buy the property and I didn't have a pony. My mother did knit the jersey but she made the neck too small, it was painful to pull over my head. My mother said no it wasn't and to stop making a fuss. Whatever my mother said, she meant, every word. On account, perhaps, of being a poet.

She didn't publish her poems. For one, she had her work cut out being a mother. Never, she was proud of announcing, had she left her children with a babysitter.

For two, she was teaching me to be a poet. At Christmas other kids left Brazil nuts for Santa. I was to leave . . . a glass of sherry . . . a mince pie . . . an orange . . . and a verse. Santa demolished the goodies and responded in kind. So did the fairies for whom she insisted I deposit a ballad, on Midsummer Eve, in the herbaceous border. Next day I found a clutch of rhyming couplets, a little brown tin mare (Woolworth's one and six) and a handful of Cadbury's chocolate fingers. Poetry was magic. Poetry worked.

For three, poetry was something – like showing emotion, wiping your nose on your sleeve, masturbating – to which you didn't ever admit. Not to strangers. It was something everyone did, though. In my home it was the norm that when you were a bit low or lonely or simply had an hour to spare, you nipped upstairs and dashed off a saga to rival *Noggin the Nog*. But when I tried to cash in on my efforts by writing the first part of a serial and persuading all and sundry to cough up a penny for the next episode Mum was furious.

Mum also taught me logic. Every single impulse from Monday

morning tummy to a mad dash along the beach to fling myself into her arms could be sorted out by sitting down with her and calmly exploring why I felt as I did. Which might be splendid training for a poet. Or a philosopher. Not much cop in a child's world, though. At kindergarten when one of the boys snatched my xylophone-playing Toby dog on wheels I assured him I could quite see why he wanted to borrow Toby. He could have him for five minutes, then I would have him for five. I was a weirdo.

The trouble with logic is it leaves no room for feelings. There were no wild griefs in my childhood home, no rages, no outbursts of passionate joy, no urgent excursions on to Mum's lap to smother her face with kisses. All such desires, once carefully discussed, could be traced to too late and too cheesy a supper; a particularly nasty outbreak of bullying; or overexcitement which would, if I wasn't careful, lead to tears before bed.

One day there were tears before I got up. It was my birthday and I can't imagine why I was allowed to open my presents in bed; perhaps I was recovering from chicken-pox?

The presents were just wonderful! There was a huge, home-made teddy bear who emerged from his wrappings clutching a poem about the magic spells he'd weave. There was a brand new book in a shiny, yellow cover – its pages smelt like marzipan – and two second-hand ones (the Secret Seven, Milly-Molly-Mandy) which I'd especially wanted. There was a tin of biscuits. And there was Twinkle Dee. My mother had stitched him in the image of the elf from my favourite fairy tale: with exquisite attention to the details of his long, green pointed hat; the thin, red belt buckled round his waist; the pinked hem of his elf-skirt; and the round, silver bells tinkling on his velvet boots. I had been given, for my birthday, all the magic my mother could conjure.

I looked at the wrapping paper at the bottom of the bed and felt something which wasn't either Monday morning tummy or the urge to hug my mum. I looked again. I thought perhaps if I were to tear up all the paper? But we always folded it and used it again next year. I reached down and mussed it a little, giving each piece a timid, petulant tap; but didn't make even the smallest hole in the paper. I flopped back on to the pillow.

It was a bright day for January; oblong slices of sun from the windows crossed my bed with bars of yellow light. Dust motes, stirred up by my mussing, drifted in the brightness. My thick, brown blanket smelt musty like an old cat; would I feel better, as I often did, if I picked out the black strands with my nails, one by one, from its thick weave?

I began to cry.

My mother came back, sunny from her preparations for my day.

'Ready to get up?'

I burrowed under the blanket.

'I thought we'd . . .' She launched into a list of treats.

'I've been crying.'

She stopped. 'What about?'

'I don't know.'

She didn't settle on the bed to explore and explain my grief. Instead, 'You've ruined it,' she announced. 'I was going to cook lamb chops. With tinned carrots. We were going to have treacle pudding.'

'Can't we still?'

'Not now you've been crying. You've spoiled the day.'

'We can still have the pudding.'

'It won't be the same.'

It's years later. I live three thousand miles from my mother, in America. I'm married. And I've received my birthday letter.

My husband knows the drill and opens the envelope. I watch him as he reads. I feel as I used to at the start of each university term on the evening before I left home. Monday morning tummy in reverse.

All day I avoided my mother, ironing and packing as unobtrusively as I could. Come the evening I dared to hope that I would get away with it. But there always came the point when I had to close my trunk; and prepare for bed. That was her cue to slip into the room with a bright, innocent, 'All ready then?' and settle for the going-away chat. At first the chat was nostalgic; it featured our good times in the hols and how much she'd enjoyed me being home; then it veered towards how empty the house would seem; it descended into melancholy.

My husband has finished reading. 'Is it as bad as I think?' I ask.

He nods.

'Does she still have the bit about the jasmine?'

He nods again.

'I'd better see it.'

The letter reads, as birthday letters always do, 'xx years ago, just after you were born, I held you in my arms. The winter jasmine was blooming outside the window and I was so pleased to have my new daughter. These days I might as well have no daughter . . .' Then there's a list of my faults. It's a long list, but I know my biggest fault is that I have left her; that's why the scent of jasmine, these days, reduces her to tears.

She isn't crying – of course not – for a live daughter. 'You might as well be dead,' she writes. My mother is bereaved of her children; and bereavement has turned to anger. Anger of such force it stretches across the Atlantic, cutting into my flesh like a rubber band pulled tight.

On the eve of another childhood birthday (one when I was well), my mother took me into the back room where my presents – as yet unwrapped – lay on the dining table, shrouded in a sheet. 'Stand still,' she instructed. She took a corner of the cover and whisked it up. I saw a jumble of brightly coloured toys; then the sheet was replaced. 'They're *all* for you,' she promised. These days she lifts the lid only on things I don't want to see.

*

It's the early eighties. There's a tube strike, bus strike, rail strike; whatever the cause, there is no easy way out of London. My mother has died. My sister and I must reach Devon (where she has died) that night.

The car I am driving is my dad's. It's a brand new, dark blue Mini Metro. Dad's lent me it because he can't drive, his eyesight's bad. I can't drive either. For years – in America – I've had automatics and have no idea how to change gear, much less do a hill start. We follow the South Circular; the South Circular's *all* hills. On a particularly long one I am terrified that I will slide backwards, cause an accident, damage the car. How will that look? An accident on the way to my mother's funeral! Later, in Devon, my fear is far worse; I'm driving my dad and my sister to the funeral itself and Devon is hillier even than the South Circular. Will I smash, by mistake, into the car behind? And spoil the day?

We arrive in Devon in one piece, but late. Too late to do anything but go to bed. Next morning, at the nursing home, we hurry to my mother's room. The bed is empty. I look around, half expecting to see her sitting in a chair. Perhaps she hasn't died after all? Don't be silly, they must have . . . 'laid her out' is the term, isn't it? elsewhere. A brisk attendant enters. Oh, no, she says, she's gone. How can she be? Gone where? To the undertaker's, of course. Why? Why without our permission? Hadn't we paid for the week? Apparently they need the bed.

On the way to the undertaker's, between worrying about hill starts, I demanded of myself: how could I do such a dreadful thing? To be late for my mother when she was dead?

The undertaker's was closed. I leant on the bell. Movement within, then the door opened. A man in a shiny black suit with a sombre expression explained that they weren't really open on Saturday morning.

'Where is my mother?'

He asked for particulars. Ah yes, Mum was in the Chapel of Rest, he assured me as he ushered us into his office. He'd be happy to take the time to run through the details, suggest the hymns we'd like for Mum.

'I want to see her.'

Mum wasn't ready to be seen, he explained, she'd only arrived the night before. Much better to view her later when she was prepared; and perhaps there was someone – a relative of Mum's – who could say a few words in the church on everyone's behalf?

'She's *not* your mum. Where is she?'

She was in a room out back. She was lying on a table with a purple cloth pulled up to her chin. Thin, grey hair trailed over the edge of the table. Her false teeth were missing. Her mouth was open. At her feet was a shabby altar with two crosses and a tarnished bronze vase of plastic flowers. I shut the door on the undertaker. The moment was intense: and private, like a lovers' meeting. My feelings had no name that I know of: weren't feelings, were impulses. The impulse to touch: I bent and kissed her. The impulse to hold: I put my arms around her, gathered her up. The impulse to howl.

Like a wolf. Like a coyote. Like a hyena with hysterics. The undertaker must have found the noise extraordinary; or perhaps this is common behaviour among the bereaved? Say this for him, he didn't intervene, though I went on for ages: until whatever had prompted me solidified into a determination to have things the way *I* wanted them.

I opened the door. 'Get rid of the crosses. She's not Catholic. And the plastic flowers; we'll bring our own, you can stay open. She needs a fresh nightie, not that horrible cloth. Oh and what's the smell?'

'Smell?'

'Do you apply preservative? Or is it some sort of natural process? Gases in the stomach, say?'

I wanted to know absolutely everything I could.

The professionals of mortality – the woman at the nursing home, the doctor, the undertaker, the people in the office where I registered my mother's death – seemed surprised at my interest. Why? Fair enough, it was all in a day's work for them; she was nothing out of the ordinary, was the right age to, as they put it, 'pass on'. But I only ever had one mother. So while they wanted to 'cushion the blow' by making everything smooth and easy and quiet, I wanted to be hit over and over with the fact that she was gone.

The other problem with the professionals – they knew how things should be done: the documentation, the signatures, even what form of words should be used in church and in addressing the chief mourners. I, the bereaved, was an amateur; and amateurs are ignorant.

I wasn't going to accept that. I might not achieve the sort of send-off *they'd* think right for your average mother, but I was going to make it right for mine. The right hymns, the right flowers, the right food and drink at the party afterwards. And the right clothes.

That afternoon I stood in my mother's kitchen, poking with a long-handled wooden spoon at a huge saucepan of boiling black liquid and trousers. Mum would have been furious at my staining both spoon and pot; but it was high summer in a seaside town and there were only white trousers in the shops. I was determined to wear trousers; I was going to look like myself.

Instead I looked like her.

The trousers didn't come out quite right: they weren't exactly black, but a harsh, slightly smudged, charcoal grey. And, as I said, the funeral wasn't quite right either, in spite of all the preparations. A clap of thunder striking through the Muzak, a stench of brimstone seeping beneath the apricot curtain – touches like that would have made all the difference.

After the party I had to get back to work. Immediately. Not that I was missed; a civil servant is hardly indispensable. But I needed to be doing, moving. Now.

I drove home, exceeding the speed limit, not giving hill starts a thought.

Behind the wheel of a car it is possible – one of the few places where it is these days – to feel the reality of time passing: to appreciate the exact equation between minutes and miles. As in eighty miles per hour, ninety miles per hour, a hundred. Time becomes a one-way journey; if you've passed a sign reading 'London 134' then you've passed it, simple as that. You cannot play the scene over and over.

Elsewhere, time is presented as continuum. We watch familiar commercials on TV or repeats of programmes: as though time can easily be wound back. Ads for holidays or fashions talk about where we'll be going, what we'll be wearing *this* year; as though it were no different from the last. Each night my digital alarm measures time; and delivers the hours of sleep I've ordered, just as the milkman delivers pintas. If I want more, I can change my order.

Forget alarm clocks, forget wristwatches, forget pendulums, candle clocks, sundials. Forget the 'time sponsored by Accurist', the pips that precede the news on Radio Four, the bongs that come before *News at Ten*. Measure time by the events of life: of birth and death. The thought was enough to press my foot on the accelerator almost to the floor.

Back at home I opened the A4 envelope and began on my mother's poems. After the first one, the pony one – which had sadness embedded in its dreams like nostalgia in reverse – they were all downright miserable. They featured love lost, life wasted, dreams thwarted. In retrospect, from what I can remember, I think they may also have been rather good. But they upset me so much that I stuffed them back in the envelope, then into the back of some cupboard I never used. Quite recently, when I decided to dig them out, I found they'd gone. I hope I didn't throw them away by mistake.

Back at work I found, to my surprise, that I functioned as 'normal'. No outbursts, no tears, no primitive emotions showing through. I put that down to – congratulated myself on – the sensible, thorough way I'd 'handled' things, given free rein to my 'grief'. So what if I felt, more and more, my mother behind my facial expressions, peeking through the way I walked, sat, stood? I was pleased with these glimpses. It was as if she were, without anyone else knowing, still alive.

I told myself, as though it were a secret between us, that she would be proud of the person I now was: adult, sensible and holding down a good job.

Not so proud, perhaps, of my private life. Hitherto I'd used the language and the logic she'd taught me. Problems with my husband, disagreements with friends were matters for careful thought, for logical discussion. I was fair and equable and open minded: I quite saw the fault might be mine.

Not any more.

My mother died with her anger still intact. Burning so strong it couldn't be consumed by flames. No matter that no visible fury erupted from her coffin as it slipped behind the curtain. The anger had already left her: and entered me as I howled over her unkempt corpse in the undertaker's shabby back room. Her anger became my demon. My mother possessed me. She took me over.

Or that's my story. How else to account for the way I – she – now behaved?

She wouldn't put up with my husband any more. She chased him from top to bottom of the house in wild, unpractised rage; then left him. She descended on my friends in torrents of tears. She bent anyone's and everyone's ear about my marriage. She didn't mention her own death, though.

Next she found a new lover. She was horrible to him: angry, truculent, passionate by turns. Neither he nor I knew what to expect. My evenings, once grey and flat, became turbulent seas, volcanic landscapes: sex and violence and raw, unspecified emotion erupted in tidal waves or ripped through the thin topsoil of acceptable behaviour.

My mother was opinionated, was, to quote my ex-husband, 'rumbunctious'. She lost quite a few of my friends that way. 'Oh, there she goes,' they'd say, 'off on one of her hobby horses. Quick, change the subject.'

My mother was visited by irrational fears and phobias. A pathological terror of spiders which I'd had when I was a child and which she'd calmly talked me out of. A dread of the dead birds my cat brought in. Of mice. Of snails. Of dentists. Fears so strong that even a glimpse of their triggers could turn her hysterical.

I never knew what next she would lose, disorder or destroy. She dropped my bag and let its contents spill across the pavement; she lost my keys so I had to stay overnight in a hotel; at work she made sudden, unsuitable remarks; at home she blundered into things and broke them. I felt like an adolescent, gripped by her violent, unpredictable desires.

The impulses were alien, yet I couldn't stop acting on them. I was a mere observer of what I did. God knows how many people's days, around that time, I spoiled.

Of course, my mother was still a stickler for saying what she meant. When she felt bad she said so. When she felt good – as more and more now, she did – she said so too. And when she felt nothing . . .

I was at my sister's. My smallest niece asked – in the way kids do – 'Mary, do you love me?' I'd never used the verb: not to my mother, my husband, my lover. I had a feeling it might be important to keep it for some special occasion not just toss it back, like a ball, to a child in search of reassurance. I thought for a moment, then came up with, 'I don't know.' Added hastily and honestly, 'I do like you, though.' Small wonder that my niece collapsed in tears. My response was as weird as the one I'd made, back in kindergarten, to the boy who'd snatched Dog Toby.

The time came when I couldn't trust my mother in the office. I swapped the civil service for a job in which everyone was volatile, the occasional outburst was *de rigueur*. At weekends I/she had tantrums and argued and fucked a lot. I grew used to her ruling the roost; would wake with a touch of excitement wondering what on earth she/I'd get up to today.

I don't really know when my feelings stopped being my mother's and started to become mine. I don't know because there wasn't a single identifiable instant, an epiphany like the moment I entered the Chapel of Rest. The nearest I can come to such an occasion is during a course at work on stress management.

'Stress,' announced the workshop leader, 'can be defined as an inappropriate reaction to an event, emotional or otherwise.' If something made you angry, she went on, and you didn't express the anger, you were under stress. If something made you want to leap for joy and you kept both feet firmly on the ground, you were under stress. How very, very simple! I had been, all the years of my mother's life, 'under stress'. And now I wasn't.

No, the nearest I can come to such an occasion is the day I dyed my hair. My mother's hair was beautiful, a rich, jet black which English people rarely have. Once mine was too; now it was fading. So I dyed it black, as I had dyed the trousers for her funeral. Like the trousers, my hair didn't come out quite right; it was harsh, artificial, dead, with no softness to it. It didn't look like Mum's hair and it didn't look like mine. What should my hair look like? I'd always wanted, even when I was ten and wanted a pony, to have a long blonde mane. Well why not?

I was used, these days, to acting on impulse; and to finding, when I did, that the sky did not fall in, people's days weren't spoilt. Or if it did, if they were, then that was God's or their lookout. I took myself off to the hairdresser's and spent a fortune on straw-coloured highlights. They were terrific. My lover said so. My colleagues said so. Everyone said so. My mother, had she been alive, would have said so too. No knowing that she mightn't have wanted to have exactly the same thing done.

No knowing because somewhere between her dying and the dyeing of my hair, my mother had 'passed' as they say, 'peacefully away'. This time there was no shock, no fright, no turmoil. My mother – in her role as demon – had vented her anger to the full; and moved on to emotions of equal depth but a damn sight pleasanter. She had tasted her oysters, both real and imagined; now she was comfortably tired, ready to take the weight off her feet. It is tempting to think that by allowing her to possess me I gave her the chance, finally, to get some rest.

And tempting to think that she, in her turn, had brought me to an adulthood which was all my own.

A postscript. The other Sunday a gang of us were sitting around in my front room considering two earth-shattering topics: 'The worst haircut in the world' and 'How I would like to be seen by other people'. My mates reached a gratifying conclusion on the second point: were they to meet me for the first time they would conclude that I was 'something creative'. I put that down to the long, streaky blonde hair, the jeans, the trainers, the Bruce Springsteen T-shirt. Then I remembered the haircut to end all haircuts. Delving into a drawer I produced a snap taken by a civil service photographer – for a security pass – just before my mother's death.

The picture is of a blank-eyed, dark-haired young woman, immobile, shoulders hunched. You can't see her hands, but you can tell by her upper body posture that they are neatly folded in her lap. She looks as though she's in a waiting room – not waiting for anything scary like the doctor or the dentist or a birthday letter. She's waiting to be admitted.

Opinion on the haircut was unanimous. The hair was short and flat on top. The sides were smoothed down. Stubby ducktails protruded from beneath each ear. A single cowlick commaed on the forehead. The cowlick was much too short to be the one on the nursery rhyme girl who was either very very good or horrid. This curl was nothing definite; and it presided over a pale, indefinite face.

Everyone agreed it was a *dreadful* haircut.

What *was* in question was the identity of the person in the pic. 'That can't be you!' 'If you'd shown it to me cold I'd never have known.' 'I can see the resemblance, but it's only a family one. I'd never have said it was you.' 'It could be a younger brother perhaps?' The person in the pic is how I looked before I became my mother.

I hope I find my mother's poems soon. I'd like to read them. Not as a child, awed into silence by her magic. Not as a daughter, recoiling from her anger. Not as herself, feeding bereavement with the fuel of self-pity. But as a woman reading, with interest, what another woman wrote.

S H E I L A   M A C L E O D

It is Margaret You Mourn For

Trying to recall the circumstances of my mother's death, I remembered 1973 as a terrible year, one of those which seems jinxed from the start and drags leadenly on, stubborn and athwart. The sky was unvaryingly grey, summer and winter, without a shaft of sun, a drop of rain, a breath of wind. And I was always standing at a bus stop, reading one Iris Murdoch novel after another in a doomed attempt to shut out the reality of the present, on my twice-daily way to and from the hospital where my eight-year-old son was recovering all too fitfully from a broken shoulder. Meanwhile, in another hospital miles away in Wales, my mother was undergoing a mastectomy and radiation treatment, and I could never get away to see her. All was frustration, anxiety, stasis.

When I looked up the relevant volume of my diary I was taken aback by the inaccuracy of my memory. Not only was the summer blazingly hot but the temperature was well into the seventies by the end of March. Far from being static, this was a year crowded with events, including moving house, to the extent that I felt buffeted by them. My son was already out of hospital by the time my mother went in, and I did go to see her. I gave her a copy of *My Friend Says It's Bullet-Proof* (a novel about a woman coping with mastectomy) and we sat in the sun in the hospital grounds, talking of this and that, being positive about the future. This was in August and I didn't believe she was going to die, let alone that it would be in less than four months' time.

My unverified memory may have been weak on facts but it was nevertheless unassailably strong in emotional truth. 1973 was a year of frustration, anxiety and disaster, in which I was continually being torn in all directions, trying to be all things to all people. And in spite of my determination to find cause for optimism, disaster remained an ever-present, insidious whisper in my ear, like the buzz of an insect brushed irritably aside, only to return again and again.

When my sister Helen called me to say that our mother had died, I experienced a split-second of absolute terror, absolute panic, and immediately became calm. I even wrote in my diary that the news had been expected, although this was at best a half-truth. I had not expected my mother to die (she was only fifty-seven) and for years could neither accept nor wholly believe that she actually was dead; but at the same time I wasn't surprised that something so terrible should have happened. The whole year had been leading to this final devastation. Now, like my mother's suffering, it was over. It seemed at the time that I too felt nothing, but I can see now that I was in shock and clamped by the pain of numbness.

In the big remote outside world Mr Heath's government was in trouble: there were strikes, power cuts and the possibility of the three-day week was about to become a reality. The West End show in which my then husband, Paul, was starring was suddenly threatened with closure after a matter of weeks, although the cast had been all set for at least a year's run. The management refused to allow their star a couple of days off to attend his mother-in-law's funeral in the Outer Hebrides, where she had been born and had asked to be buried. But when Paul, to my eternal gratitude, stood firm, they had to cave in.

It was nearly thirty years since my parents, my sisters and I had left the Isle of Lewis. I had been back briefly ten or eleven years earlier with Paul when we were both students, visited my grandparents (both of whom had since died) and spent a few happy summer days on the long, empty, silvery beaches. Now we were back again in the depths of winter with Helen and my father and my mother's coffin. It was a different place. I was a different person. And yet the moment we set foot on the island everyone knew who we were and what we were there for. Although no one was actually intrusive, I found this unnerving.

The funeral took place at the house in Garrabost where my mother had been born, the tenth of eleven children. All my mother's family were tall and blond, but she was short and dark and often referred to herself as 'the runt of the litter' (although at other times she claimed with pride to be the double of Deanna Durbin). Her own mother had died a few years earlier at the age of ninety-eight, I had been mildly shocked by the equanimity with which my mother had received the news: 'Her life had become a burden to her.' It was her sister Katie, who had been like a mother to her, for whom my mother had truly grieved. Only twice before had I seen her so stricken: at the death of my eleven-month-old sister; and (this is one of my earliest memories) as she read by the light of an oil lamp the telegram which announced that her brother John had been killed in the war. Now the surviving brothers and sisters had all left the island, except for my Uncle Torquil who lived alone in the Garrabost house and was in the process of turning the surrounding land into a sheep ranch.

The service was conducted in both English and Gaelic, the unaccompanied Gaelic psalms sung in the form of call and response and sounding ancient, strangely Middle Eastern. As was customary, only the men went with the bier to the cemetery while the women stayed behind to prepare the funeral tea. There was a general sense of shock that my mother should have died so young and a consensus that my father had been expected to 'go' first, he being ten years older, and male to boot. I hadn't noticed, until Helen pointed it out, that I was replying in English to questions addressed to me in Gaelic. I had assumed until then that I understood not one word of the language, so this was a further oddity, a further dislocation.

One of my aunts told how she and my mother used to sit on the sands into the long summer evenings, watching the ships that came to collect the young men to go and work on farms in Canada. The Canadian farmers met the ships and chose the most stalwart men as their farmworkers, while the weakest were left homeless and penniless. From there the talk passed to the Highland Clearances and it seemed, by the immediacy with which they were evoked, that they had taken place only a few years ago. But mostly the talk was of family, its members now dispersed throughout the world, making new lives for themselves in England, Canada, Australia or South Africa. All this interconnection in both time and space was something I could perceive but not feel. History, geography, human life were, rather, a series of brutal disjunctions, of which death was only the last.

It wasn't until the next day that Helen and I could visit the cemetery at Aignish where our mother was buried. There had been a storm during the night and the site, on the narrowest isthmus of land, seemed horribly vulnerable to the wind and the lashing sea on either side. Paul said it was beautiful, but to me it was a place without mercy and, if it belonged to God, then He was a God of wrath. But I didn't believe in any god, let alone one who had gathered my mother to his bosom. There were only the elements –and extinction.

The plane wasn't due to leave until the afternoon, so we had time to visit the schoolhouse at Cromore where Helen and I were both born. I had never been back since I had left it at the age of five, and inwardly prepared myself for disappointment, at the same time steeling myself against a possible inundation of memories. I found a large, solid stone house, the school now a tea-room and the garden on three sides sloping down to the shores of Loch Erisort. Everywhere the views were of water and across water to the opposite shore, a misty strip of indigo appearing and disappearing again in the dramatic weather. The place was so beautiful as to hold me there in the present, a tourist. There were no ghosts, no skeletons emerging from cupboards, just a pleasant sense of astonishment that Helen and I should have come from *here*.

When we got to the airport there was no plane: it had never arrived from Glasgow, and the pilot wasn't even going to decide for another two hours whether he would take off at all because of the cross-winds. The next morning at nine o'clock we were still waiting, sitting in our hired car at the deserted 'drome' with snow swirling around us and the engine running to keep us warm. The radio news was full of Mr Heath's speech to the nation, announcing the three-day week and a rise in petrol prices. It would, said one commentator, be the worst Christmas since the war. Hours passed and it began to seem that we would never be able to leave the island. It was all, we told each other, horribly symbolic.

Eventually we got seats on the Loganair plane which had come from Glasgow with the newspapers. It took eight passengers and we flew with the doors open. We could see the cemetery in its tiny strip and the house at Garrabost. Lewis gave way to a chain of other islands, the links becoming smaller and smaller. Then we were flying above the clouds in the sun, and the pilot radioed Glasgow to ensure that we would make our connection to London. It was the last day of the school term. The show was still running in the West End. Back to normal. The nightmare was over.

But it had hardly yet begun. There is a joke definition of a Scotsman (or is it a Highlander?) which for me comes near the bone: someone who receives a joke solemnly and the next day can be heard laughing at it in his bath. My upbringing did not encourage spontaneity, distrusted the overt expression of emotion. By education I was trained to be analytical and sceptical. And I learned early on that self-control was the supreme virtue, especially for the female of the species. I went back dutifully to my duties, telling myself that nothing I felt or said or did could help my mother, would bring her back to me. But over the following eighteen months and with increasing rapidity, I found myself falling to pieces.

Grief may have many faces but most of them are wearing masks. I knew that when I wept I mourned, but when I raged I felt I was doing something else: demanding justice, perhaps, or setting the record straight. A nurse at the hospital had told Helen that everyone involved had known all along that our mother's was a terminal case. The mastectomy and radiotherapy alike had been futile, and were known to be so. I was furious that my mother should have been put through all that unnecessary suffering. Why couldn't they just have left her alone? It was wicked to be so dishonest as to give people false hope in order to salve medical conscience.

There were plenty of people to be angry with, including my mother herself, and I ran through them all in turn. It felt good to have someone to accuse or blame, in however small a part. At the same time I was full of a manic energy which, curiously, people seemed to find attractive, thus reinforcing my behaviour. I say curiously, because even at the time I knew this glittering extrovert to be a fraud and her busy, supercompetent social life a desperate distraction. But from what? That was a question I was unable to face, with an answer I was unable to pinpoint.

The public persona had a private obverse: a wretched creature given to uncontrollable fits of weeping for no apparent reason and increasingly convinced of her own uselessness as a wife, a mother, a human being. I took anti-depressants as prescribed, stopped for fear of becoming addicted, then started again because I seemed not to be able to cope without them. And so it went on. All this time I had the sensation of leading a posthumous existence, haunting my own life like a wandering, unappeasable ghost. That I had lost about twenty pounds in weight only added to the feeling of insubstantiality.

Such was the persona I hid from the world and did my best to hide from my children. I was both caught and lost between it and the good-time girl. Something had to give. In the summer of 1974 my father asked me to sort out my mother's clothes, separating the discards from those which could be passed on to some charitable jumble sale. My instinctive reaction was to shrink from the task, but I agreed with apparent readiness, suspecting that he couldn't bear to do it himself. As I threw out garment after garment, each one stained in exactly the same place, I experienced a mounting sense of horror and a need (which I suppressed) to howl and scream. It was as if it was my mother I was throwing away. As I wrote in my diary at the time, the process seemed an interminable ordeal but in fact lasted only two hours. They were two hours in which my defences were completely eroded and the manic extrovert sent whimpering into oblivion.

One day I found I couldn't get out of bed because my legs were paralysed. When the doctor was called and examined me, he could find nothing wrong, apart from the obvious fact that I was under-weight. He asked me if there had been any great sorrow in my life. The phrase sticks in mind because it seemed so quaintly old-fashioned – and yet so right. He prescribed tranquillisers and I could walk again. It was only days later that I remembered my mother say-ing, the last time I saw her, 'My legs are so weak they won't carry me upstairs.'

I had known dimly all along that when I felt like a ghost I was in some way identifying with my mother, in some sense taking her death upon myself and as my own. In the same way I had known too that when I was the life and soul of the party I was fleeing from any such identification, reclaiming what seemed to be the fact of my own identity, the fact of my own life. I saw now that my behaviour was saying: my mother is dead and I am alive. And that the guilt involved in this assertion (however true) was just too much to bear.

Inevitably when I talked about my mother at this time, people would ask me, 'Were you very close?' The question seemed oddly inappropriate, like a ball being kicked on to the pitch from a neigh-bouring game, and I would usually reply along the lines of, 'No – that was just the problem.' This half-truth was the best I could manage. It was true that my mother and I were not close in the sense of seeing a lot of each other, of exchanging confidences, or even of having very much to talk about whenever we were together. But, as my behaviour had underlined, it was also true that in another elusive and more profound sense we were close indeed, too close for comfort.

When I was a very little girl I thought my mother the most wonderful person in the world and could hardly bear to let her out of my sight. I remember quite consciously being tormented by jealousy when my sister Helen was born, and I also remember it becoming a matter of pride to pretend otherwise. When I said to my mother, who was nursing Helen at the time, 'Put that thing in the pram and come and play with me', the wish and emotion betrayed were received by my parents as a huge joke, and one which was to be recounted unrelentingly in the family for years to come. Ridicule should not be underrated as a weapon for effecting repression.

My mother managed the situation by engaging me as her ally, her little helper who would run to fetch the nappy-pin or see that baby didn't fall out of the high-chair. And I suppose that with the birth of each succeeding sister (there are five of us) I became ever more helpful, ever more motherly and (so my sisters tell me) ever more bossy. Just before the birth of my third sister the doctor who had come to visit my mother asked me what I wanted to be when I grew up. 'An expectant mother,' I answered promptly, having just read the government-issued booklet of that title.

Throughout my childhood I was always the one in charge of the others, taking them to and from school or babysitting when my parents went out. I took my duties seriously, carrying them out to the letter. Maybe I was afraid of reprisal, which would have come from my father, but I also wanted to please and be praised: to please my mother and be praised by her. As I remember, praise of this sort usually came from neighbouring women who told my mother how lucky she was to have such a daughter, 'little mother' that I was myself. I could never tell whether she agreed with them or not.

My mother would often stare at me and say, 'What a strange child you are', or, 'What a curious profile you have', or, 'I am the cat that walked by itself and all places are alike to me.' I was puzzled by those and other similar remarks and, dismissing my unease at being described as a solitary oddity, fooled myself into accepting them as compliments. My mother was always right and, if I was strange, then I would make a virtue of it.

Often it seemed she knew, not so much what I was thinking, but exactly what I was feeling, homing in on my secret doubts and fears with uncannily intuitive accuracy. Two such moments remain fixed in my memory like epiphanies. In the first it is autumn and I am eight or nine years old. I am standing at the french windows, staring out at the garden while I clutch and unclutch the austerity curtains made out of parachute silk with a camouflage pattern. What I am feeling, as I watch the leaves fall, is inexpressible. Then I hear my mother's voice behind me: 'Margaret, are you grieving/Over Goldengrove unleaving?' She recites the whole poem through to its last line: 'It is Margaret you mourn for.' And of course (if for 'Margaret' you read 'Sheila') it is. Through the medium of Gerard Manley Hopkins, my mother has put my intimations of mortality into words. But indirectly, metaphorically, as though the secret has barely been acknowledged between us.

The second moment occurred some years later when the good little girl had metamorphosed into an adolescent horror and I had been anorexic for a couple of years. My mother succeeded in getting through to me by quoting a poem of William Blake's which begins, 'Ah, Sun-flower, weary of time . . .' and I recognised myself with a sense of shock as the 'pale Virgin shrouded in snow'. Such intuitive *rapprochements* constituted the closeness between us, the very closeness I had been fighting, in my anorexia, to deny and reject because it threatened my own fragile sense of identity. But it was also seductive, a safe, warm place where I was someone special, the eldest and (to me, the same thing) best of daughters.

Throughout my prolonged adolescence the denial and rejection were uppermost. I began to balk at running errands at my mother's behest, noting that they always involved some degree of social embarrassment which she preferred to avoid. Whenever an excuse or complaint or often even a simple enquiry had to be made to anyone outside the family, it seemed that I became my mother's representative. I resented having to lie, but even more I despised the social ineptitude which necessitated the subterfuge. Sometimes my mother would blush when addressed by a stranger, and I would be mortified to see her behave like a hick from the sticks. When she spoke on the phone she would put on a posh voice. In company she would giggle, flirt with men half her age, pretend to be feather-brained and generally rely on her good looks and charm (both of which were considerable) to get by. All this was quite beneath my adolescent contempt. When I got to her age, I vowed, I would be poised, self-assured, open and forthright as I engaged in intelligent conversation with my peers and never, ever fluttered a single, solitary eyelash.

My aspiration was to feel at home in the world, as it seemed my parents were not. I think my mother always felt like an exile. She always referred to the Isle of Lewis as 'home' and continued to read the Stornoway Gazette week after week. Gaelic was her first language and, once we had moved to England, there was no one with whom she could speak it. She would sing Gaelic songs and, although some of them were joyous and celebratory, the ones I remember most are those which seemed to throb with homesickness and loss.

In those years my main feeling about my mother was a kind of embarrassed irritation. Not only did she dwell too much on and in the past, but she would never stand up to my father. I had no use for what I perceived as her passivity, and when she bemoaned the probability that all my education would only render me unfit for marriage and motherhood, I retorted that I was damned if I was going to tune *my* life to suit some man. My mother said I would soon change my mind about that. As I duly did.

It wasn't until after the birth of my first child that our relationship became happier, attained some sort of equilibrium. Now we had something in common: real motherhood as opposed to the notional version of my childhood. Now I understood her better, and at the same time could accept the differences between us with composure, sometimes even finding in them a gratifying sense of my own singularity after all. The old ambivalences seemed to have vanished. But my reaction to her death implies that they were never properly resolved.

The root of my grief lay embedded and submerged in a feeling too terrible to contemplate: that the world was now a place bereft of mothering love for ever and ever. And yet what did I know about mothering love? It seemed to be something I had never experienced, had been hoping to claim some day, had been hoping to merit. Now that chance had been snatched from me. In the process I had been freed from the necessity of trying to be a good little girl. And I didn't know if this was a good thing or a bad one. I was reluctant to let go of that good little girl, even as I despised her.

The funeral trip to Lewis only served to emphasise the ambivalences. It seemed even at the time to be so layered with meaning as to be unreal: a film I was watching, a film trying so hard to be significant that it approached pastiche. The return to the island was like a return to a mother who wasn't there, perhaps had never been there. It was a place I had once belonged to, and yet that 'I' wasn't I at all. It was a place I had left, and yet, as we sat out the snowstorm in Stornoway aerodrome, it seemed to be somewhere I could never leave entirely, a place whose bleak, rejecting beauty would always draw me back.

But that was twenty years ago, and I haven't been back since. Perhaps I never will. And perhaps I'll go back one day with my sons and visit my mother's grave. It seems to matter less and less whether I go back or not. I don't need to be there to remember, and I don't need a headstone to remind me of my mother. Separation, once a source of distress, then of rebellion, is now complete in being revealed for what it is: a necessity and, finally, an inevitable one.

Sometimes I dream about my mother, but the one recurrent dream which haunted me for years now seems to have stopped. In it I would meet her by chance in some unexpected place, perhaps in a foreign country, always in a garden or somewhere green. But although I am surprised and overjoyed to see her, it seems that she has been expecting me, perhaps dreading my appearance. I bite back the wounding exclamation: 'But I thought you were dead!' She looks at me with a rueful half-smile and I can tell that she knows what I'm thinking. To add to my shame, she asks me, 'How could you believe such a thing?' I try to defend myself by explaining that it was my father who had told me she was dead. At which she looks more rueful, more cynical than ever, as if to say, *Et tu, Brute*. I want to know where she has been and why she has never let any of us know that she was still alive. But she only smiles mysteriously, perhaps a little mischievously. I am left wondering at the inexplicable behaviour of both my parents.

Now the dreams are less frequent and have lost their accusatory thrust. But perhaps I have got the message. It seems to me that the dead live on for as long as we remember them, that this is the life we owe them. And I think of Truffaut's last film, where the hero, keeping a candle burning for each of his remembered dead, transforms a hidden room into a blaze of light. In the hidden room I carry with me, as we all must, the candle burning the brightest is for my mother.

MAEVE BINCHY

Happy Families

When I was at school there was a girl who was called out of class one day by the nuns.

She was a very good girl, so we knew there couldn't have been any great crime involved like smoking in the cloakroom or reading a comic at spiritual reading.

Then we heard her mother had died.

At twelve she had lost her mother.

Naturally there were a lot of prayers said for the repose of her mother's soul, and we all went to the funeral as a mark of respect and saw the family in black and even grown-ups with red tear-stained faces following a coffin down the church.

I didn't know how she could bear it.

I looked at her in class and she used to laugh when the teacher made a joke, and she was able to care about whether we got homework or not. And she was able to join in singsongs with all the rest of us.

I decided she must never have loved her mother, not one bit. And in an excess of devotion to my own mother I told her this. My mother said she never heard such nonsense in her whole life. She said that the unfortunate woman who was dying, the mother of the little girl at school, would only have had one hope which was that her family would survive without her.

I listened but I didn't agree. My mother had lost her own parents very young, her mother had died at childbirth, her father when she was around four. She had grown up with a stepmother who later remarried so my mother had a stepfather as well. This must have made things more remote and distant for her, I decided; she didn't have a *real* family like we had. That's why she was so well able to take care of herself, and not be afraid of loud noises or striking up conversations with total strangers, or digging up all the roses in the garden and transplanting them to the other side where there was more sun.

My mother could do all kinds of things, like take a bone out of your throat if it got stuck and you were choking, like clean out a turkey on Christmas Eve when it arrived far from oven-ready. Like have all the relations she could find to Sunday lunch with us because she knew that Sunday was lonely in a city and that students never had any money. She would know in the fuel shortages where they were cutting down trees and go and buy logs at a penny each which she would wheel home in the pram. She could take out splinters and cure headaches and get the grocery to deliver her a packet of Gold Flake by giving a list of other items as well and asking if it could be brought up to the house soon because she was in a hurry for the cornflour. The notion of the family, the home, or the neighbourhood existing without her was so remote that it was only considered in the worst of nightmares.

Then a new girl came to the school. We were fourteen at that stage, it was 1954 and the hit song of the time was Eddie Calvert playing 'Oh Mein Papa' on his golden trumpet. But we couldn't sing it or hum it even because the new girl's father had just died. That's why she had changed schools, and she and her mother had come to live nearby in a smaller house. We used to look at her in dumb sympathy. Imagine there being no father at home to be interested in everything, to talk to about homework, to take you on outings down to Dun Laoghaire swimming baths, and buy fourpenny ice-creams instead of twopenny ones.

No father sitting at the table in the evening telling stories about people at work, people called Maurice and Kevin and Billy who were lawyers also and who had won cases or had lost them. No father bursting with pride at a good report or biting his lip with disappointment at a bad one.

And yet that was the year when Doris Day sang 'Once I had a Secret Love', and so did the rest of us who had no love at all, secret or otherwise. We sang it everywhere and so did the girl who had no father.

I decided that maybe God gave you some kind of a shell like a tortoise that made you forget that your mother or father was dead.

It would be the only thing that could explain how they could behave normally in such an abnormal situation. In Ireland then, families only lost someone by death. There was no divorce, no separation. A family without a mother or a father meant there had been a tragedy.

I used to pray very hard that it was a tragedy that would pass over our house, far away up in the sky and never settle. 'We all have to die some time,' my mother used to say in her practical way, just as if she was saying we have to buy broken biscuits rather than whole ones because this family would hoover a tin of Afternoon Tea selection empty in no time. I hated her saying we all had to die. I absolutely hated it.

'It's because you were a nurse,' I would say, furious with her. 'You got used to seeing dead people. It made you as tough as nails.'

'I never got used to talking to their relations,' my mother said. 'People could die easily and peacefully, a lot of them did, but it was heartbreaking to talk to a husband or wife or parents or children. I often had to go to the parlour in the nursing home and tell them. I never got used to that.'

In a way it was a comforting thing to say. To tell a child that people faced death without fear; it was only their relatives that wept over them.

But I still felt confused about those girls at school who had survived the death of parents so well.

We were an odd family in a way, because we all lived at home instead of leaving the nest to find nestlets of our own. It had all to do with geography, really. Our house was ten miles from Dublin City where we all went to university and then to work. Ten miles is near enough to live at home, and just a little too near to get a flat unless there was some bad feeling. And there was no bad feeling.

My memory of my home was that it was very happy, and that there was more fun and life there than there was anywhere else. So why would any of us go? And anyway I was the eldest; if anyone should have made the move, I should have made it, but there seemed no point. Why leave a good place?

There were four children.

I would have liked two older brothers who would have looked after me, taught me how to climb trees, taken me on adventures and eventually when the time came introduced me to their friends who would all fall in love with me.

It was not to be . . .

I was the big bossy older sister, full of enthusiasms, mad fantasies, desperate urges to be famous and anxious to be a saint. A settled sort of saint, not one who might have to suffer or die for her faith. I was terrified that I might see a vision like St Bernadette or the Children at Fatima and be a martyr instead. My schoolfriends accuse me of making this up but I never looked up into trees in case I saw Our Lady beckoning to me. I didn't know if there were any trees around the hockey pitch at school, I was so fearful of catching a sight of a lady in blue and white in them. I was lucky enough to be fairly quick at understanding what was taught, but unlucky enough not to be really interested in it so I always got my exams but never had the scholar's love of learning for its own sake.

And even though I was fat and hopeless at games, which are very unacceptable things for a schoolgirl, I was very happy and confident.

That was quite simply because I had a mother and a father at home who thought I was wonderful. They thought all their geese were swans. It was a gift greater than beauty or riches, the feeling that you were as fine as anyone else.

Being the eldest was hard. You had to make all the running.

I was desperately reliable. If I had to be home at ten at ten on the dot I was back. If I went away to stay with a schoolfriend in the country or with cousins, I wrote letters and sent postcards home. It was much easier for the others to forge their various ways in the world, Maeve had done it for them, shown that we could be trusted, that the sky wouldn't fall if we were allowed to leave the nest temporarily.

But they were all equally reliable so perhaps we were a very devoted, compliant family. There was no real rebellion, no aching to be free, no questioning of attitudes apart from the usual wishing to take the opposite side on any issue like musical tastes, length of skirts, hair, or politics. We never had to worry much about pains and aches at home because of our mother having been a nurse before she married and we had a good kind family doctor who was a friend, and anything like flu or jaundice or whatever was treated royally well, with the patient having a fire in the bedroom and a whole siphon of lemonade to themselves. There was a heavy emphasis on not wearing damp clothes. I remember an airing cupboard literally groaning with clothes; we were terrified to trust any garment to the wardrobes in our rooms.

And I grew up and became a schoolteacher. My mother hoped I would meet a nice doctor or barrister or accountant who would marry me and take me to live in what is now called Fashionable Dublin Four. But she felt that this was a vain hope.

I was a bit loud to make a nice professional wife, and anyway I was too keen on spending my holidays in far-flung places to *meet* any of these people. The future leaders of society did not holiday on the decks of cheap boats, or work in kibbutzim in Israel or mind children as camp counsellors in the United States. She abandoned this hope on my behalf and got great value out of my escapades in foreign parts. I wrote marvellous long rambling letters home from these trips, editing out the bits they didn't need to know, bits about falling in love with highly unsuitable foreigners. In fact my parents were so impressed with these eager letters from abroad they got them typed and sent them to a newspaper and that's how I became a writer.

In 1967 my mother had a bad back. She spent a lot of time in bed and was in poor form much of the time; traction didn't help.

It wasn't anything serious, we all said, mainly on her own reading of the situation. She was the one who knew when things were wrong, so if there was no sense of alarm then there was nothing too bad.

Maybe it was just pains and aches of middle age, she said.

She was fifty-seven. I was twenty-seven. This must be what it was. Middle age.

That year I had hoped to go on a cargo ship, but at the last moment it fell through so I went with a group of Irish schoolteachers on an educational course to an American college.

My mother came out to the airport, to say goodbye.

'Imagine getting seven weeks, all free,' she said, full of admiration. 'You really are a great organiser, you'll have seen the whole world when you're my age.'

Then she turned around to a total stranger – she was great at getting into conversations with people she didn't know – and praised me to the skies for my sense of adventure.

And I flew off on a rather confused outing.

We were all in a college campus in upstate New York learning things that weren't very relevant, sitting out in the sunshine and swimming in a big dark lake, and taking the bus to places like Poughkeepsie to drink exotic cocktails in the afternoon.

And then I got a phone call from my sister to know was it possible for me to come home because our mother had had a bad diagnosis. Those were the words she used. I remember it still; the dining hall in the afternoon, a sort of refectory, I suppose, it happened to be the place the phone call was put through to, and sun coming in a window, other people sitting about playing cards and reading.

My mother used to have a theory that those messages that went out on the radio asking someone to contact a hospital because a relative was dangerously ill were really a code. They meant the relative was dead but it was too bald and shocking to say it so they cushioned the blow.

I asked my sister whether Mummy had had an accident. Had she been knocked down by a car?

My sister, a medical student who knew that I would think that, assured me that this wasn't what had happened. She swore to me that if I couldn't get out of the course it wouldn't matter, I could come home in September as planned.

So I knew it couldn't be an accident.

And she couldn't be dead.

I began to go on automatic pilot and said I'd get home as soon as possible.

For some reason I still don't understand I never asked what the bad diagnosis was. Somehow the phrase, the technical jargon, was enough. It tided me over until I could get home and find out. A friend of mine who was on the course rented a car and drove me to New York Airport. I sat on the plane and told the air hostess that my mother had a bad diagnosis, and she held my hand.

At Dublin Airport my sisters and brother stood in tears and told me that it was cancer and that she wouldn't live until Christmas. And we didn't care who saw us, we just stood there holding on to each other.

The thing that was never going to happen was happening. One of our parents was going to die.

I remember the supper that evening. We sat around the table and made a plan.

She was not going to be told. This was a long time ago, remember.

The thinking of the time, in our part of the world anyway, was that people couldn't bear it. They couldn't look at each other and acknowledge that this was cancer of the lymph glands, inoperable, untreatable and about to end her life.

We felt that it would be three months of weeping our hearts out. And that it would be too much for her to bear.

The long goodbye.

So the solution seemed to be that we should all assume that it was something trivial from which she would recover. And that was the play we acted in the short months that followed.

Of course she knew. But I don't think she knew that *we* knew. I don't think she could have believed that a loving family could have been capable of such a heroic act of deception.

She got thinner and more frail. She had a private room and we were in and out all day. We all coped with it in our own ways.

I remember I had a small record player in my room and I used to play 'If you go to San Francisco, be sure to wear some flowers in your hair' over and over because I had never heard it when she was well and so it didn't remind me of anything in the past, and if I heard anything like 'Danny Boy' or 'Believe me if All Those Endearing Young Charms' – things she liked – on the radio I used to turn them off sharply and start talking in a very brisk tone about something else.

We were watchdogs about her visitors: we didn't let anyone in who might bring her down or acknowledge what her illness was.

And we minded my father so well. That was the only good bit, I think: the huge bond of solidarity we had about looking after him. We made sure that there was never an evening that he was left alone in the house by himself to think about the future. We always managed to arrange that one of us come and collect him from the hospital so that he didn't have to leave that room on his own. And somehow there *must* be some kind of immunities that build up in your heart, because I don't think any of us thought it must be coming near the end now; when it was the end, it came both suddenly and peacefully.

And we who had never seen anyone at all dead, saw our mother who looked asleep and young and had no pain in her face, and that was wonderful. She really did look as if all the strain was gone, and Daddy said she looked like she did when he met her all those years ago in the sunshine in the West of Ireland.

At her funeral I looked around the crowded church and I thought I can't *bear* it, I don't believe any of this bit about May the Angels come out and Greet her and lead her into Paradise. If I did then it would be fine, she was just gone for a bit. Did everyone else believe it?

They seemed to be accepting it anyway.

I looked at my father's face, as he knelt there in his dark overcoat and his black tie, his face a uniform grey colour with lines of loneliness etched into it and I thought that for me at any rate no day was ever going to be as bad as this one, because I would never again have to look at such naked grief. When he died the grief would be my own, and I'd just have to try and get over it myself in some way or other.

I wondered what my mother would do if she were there, how she would cheer him.

She would have been practical.

So I was practical.

I reminded him of everyone's names when they came to sympathise, I put some vodka in his orange juice. He was a man who had the odd glass of sherry or a half of beer but didn't drink in any real sense of the word.

He had an awful headache the next day, which he found inexplicable but it had certainly helped him through what would have been a terrible ordeal. He was shy, no good at gatherings, he would have been looking around everywhere for her to ease the social situation. I never had any regrets about the vodka.

And life went on.

A very different life.

I thought of my mother a lot. I tried to remember the good, the funny, the laughs, the pride. But I kept thinking too of the disappointment I had been to her in so many ways: bad school reports, loud yet lazy, desperate to be noticed. And I had one huge regret – I had never taken her on a holiday. I was so anxious to see the world that I wanted to see I didn't ever pick up any hints about how nice it might have been to do a coach tour of Scotland.

Scotland! When I wanted to see India, or Turkey.

It was too late. I couldn't make it up to her. I didn't believe that she was up there in Heaven looking down approvingly. I wished I did, because then I could have sort of talked to her, but it just wasn't on.

So I decided that this would never happen with my father. I would most definitely take him on a holiday. I wouldn't be so selfish again.

My father was a busy lawyer, a barrister who always feared taking time off from his work, so I consulted the solicitors who sent him work. I told them I was thinking of taking him on a holiday on this date and perhaps they would conspire with me in telling him things weren't too urgent. They all thought this was a great idea.

My father didn't like planes, and a new ferry service from Ireland to the continent had just begun so I booked a great trip back to places he had loved when he was young.

Glowing with a halo of doing the right thing this time anyway, I showed him the tickets.

By now I was a journalist and earning a bit more than I did as a teacher, but these tickets involved much consultation with the Credit Union . . . it would be worth it of course when he had a great time.

He looked at me sadly. He didn't want to go, he said.

Truly, without my mother any trip would have no meaning for him. It would only be a constant reminder that he wanted her with him to see these places they had once been to but never again since they had a family to spend their money and time on.

'Wouldn't it be nice with me, different of course but nice?' I begged. I wanted it, needed it just as much as I had believed he did.

He was so kind as he let me know he felt too old, he felt too sad to go to places he might have gone with my mother.

He was barely sixty and he felt old.

I told him it was fine, I could get the money back. I told him I didn't mind at all and that it was great to be so frank and honest with each other.

And he believed me, and that was good.

And we all went on with our lives. My brother got married and my sister got married and my other sister got engaged. I had a good life as a columnist on the *Irish Times*. I still lived at home, we still planned our life so that our father would not be lonely. I would live at home; the others would all live nearby. There was no sense of being trapped.

My father sometimes looked long into the flames of the fire thinking about all that he had lost. Sometimes I would jolly him along, but other times I let him think.

If I wanted to go off on some roistering outing, I could. After all I was thirty-two now. Old enough to live my own life.

We were all qualified and doing well. Sometimes my father said it was a tragedy that our mother hadn't lived to see a journalist, a doctor, a social worker and a lawyer emerge from the chaos she had presided over when we were all young and troublesome.

Then one summer's day I went down to the country to interview an eccentric but interesting Irish-American millionaire about the state of Irish tourism. I stayed at his luxury castle hotel because he was flying in early next morning to be interviewed over breakfast. He told me I could invite a companion, so my best friend for many years, who was also eager to sample the hotel, came and we were given two amazing turret rooms.

I telephoned my father after dinner. I told him there was little hope of my landing a millionaire in this hotel, they were all asleep over their *Herald Tribunes*.

'Maybe you're as well off without one,' he said cheerfully. Any dealings I've ever had with them in the Law, they seem to be fractious and peevish. That wouldn't suit you at all.'

He told me that he had been playing a game of Scrabble with one of my sisters, the other had been on the phone ten minutes ago and my brother had called earlier in the evening. Sometimes you graft things on afterwards but I do distinctly remember thinking as I went up the stairs to the turret bedroom that it was good to be part of a family that kept in touch automatically, not from any sense of duty.

It was no sweat to ring my father, he would have funny anecdotes about something that had happened in court. I pitied my friends who said it was impossible to talk to their parents.

I got a phone call at 1 a.m.: could I come back? The same sister having to break bad news yet again.

This time she said she had gone into the sitting room and seen him sitting asleep in front of the television.

'Aha,' she had said. 'And *you're* the man who says he never falls asleep in front of a television programme!'

He had died of a massive coronary in his sleep. I remember all kinds of incidentals: the hotel gave us a flask of coffee and told us a garage that would be open for us to get petrol on country roads in the middle of the night.

My best friend drove me home to the house, and the beautiful early sunrise was coming up over Dublin Bay and lighting the garden where they had loved to walk. I, who had never seen anyone dead since my mother, went up to the bedroom where he lay, and I kept saying that it had to be a mistake, he looked as if he were going to get up any minute. There wasn't a thing wrong with him.

And then I touched his hand, which was ice cold.

Lots of people don't have their parents at thirty-two. Huge numbers of people loved their parents just as much as I did. They all survived as their parents would have wished. That day I honestly didn't think I would.

There were so many terrible things to be done . . . Tell my sister, who was on her honeymoon. Tell my brother, who didn't have a phone in Dundee so it meant asking a policeman to go round to the house. Tell my father's brothers, who were older than he was.

People were marvellous, as they always are and particularly so in Ireland, where nobody is afraid of intruding on your private grief. They quite correctly believe that their presence is a comfort and they come and give that comfort.

I listened again to Angels coming to lead his soul into Paradise, and I wished.

Oh I wished.

A kind colleague of his said to me that if ever a man was in Heaven it was my father. So generous with his time, so fair, so kind to everyone.

I should have said thank you and that indeed he was right, but instead I said that I didn't really go along with Heaven, so it seemed a bit bleak.

He said something that helped a lot. It mightn't help anyone else but it helped me greatly. He said: 'Surely you don't think that a great spirit like your father's and like your mother's could be snuffed out just like that. That they'd cease to exist just because they died. Do you?'

And somehow it made sense.

As long as they were remembered and referred to and thanked then they didn't totally cease to exist. That made some kind of sense, all right. But I was very very lonely when my father died.

I didn't have to support anyone, mind anyone, cheer anyone up like I had to do for him.

I used to forget he was dead. Once I sent him a postcard from Bulgaria, and only remembered when I posted it.

And I used to turn the wrong way when I came out of the *Irish Times*, thinking I was going home on the little train to our family house where I had always lived. I forgot I was taking a short bus journey to the flat where I lived on my own. Once or twice I found myself dialling him and put down the receiver with a heavy heart.

Then I decided to change everything and go to London and live a different life. It worked very well, better than I could have dreamed.

I met Gordon Snell, a writer, a man I loved, and he loved me and we got married and it was great and is still great. He believed I could do anything, just as my parents had believed all those years ago, and I started to write fiction and that took off fine.

He loved Ireland, and the fax was invented so we writers could live anywhere we liked instead of living in London near publishers. In fact they say publishers seem to *prefer* you to live miles away just as long as you have a fax . . .

So now we have this house in Dalkey a few hundred yards from the house where I lived with my parents. My sisters and brother all live nearby; we are the closest of friends. We talk of old times without any heavy emotion, we recall funny things, holidays down by the Atlantic where we used to trail our bathing suits in the water and then hang them on the clothes line to dry to let our parents think we had been for a healthy, refreshing swim.

I wish very deeply they had lived to see us all still such friends and so happy in our lives. They never saw their grandchildren, they didn't see us settle into the kind of lives they hoped for us and struggled to bring about.

But there are many days when I am grateful that they died young. They will for ever be active bright people for us. Unlike so many of our friends, we have not had to agonise about what to do when parents became frail and unable to look after themselves. We have pictures of young parents in our homes, smiling happily out of frames, not knowing that they wouldn't live to old age.

That man was right: their spirit didn't die. I would never have believed that at the time. But today I often think of them with affection and without the old bitter regret that they had to leave so early.

I wonder what they would make of my learning to drive when I was forty-nine. What would my mother think if she could see me struggling with plants that perish in a garden, when I wouldn't give two minutes of my precious time to sharing her enthusiasm for gardens all those years ago? What would my father, a near international-standard bridge player think if he saw me struggling with the game now when I wouldn't even contemplate it years ago at the time he wanted to teach it to us?

What was I *doing* that needed all this time?

I can't remember any of it.

They never knew that one of us would thank them publicly in a book. But I do like to think that they knew they gave us a great childhood, a sense of safety and home that we were able to carry with us even when they were gone.

ANDREW MOTION

Trooping Together

It's twenty years (*it's not, it's twenty-three —
be accurate*) since you were whisked away
(*I wasn't 'whisked away': I broke my skull*)
and I was left to contemplate your life.
(*My life? Ridiculous. You mean my death.*)

Well, twenty/twenty-three. I can't decide
if that's a long time or no time at all,
or whether everything I've said since then,
and thought, and done to try and work out how
the way we treat our lives might be involved
with how our lives treat us is more than just
a waste of breath. That's right. A waste of breath.

You see, you're always with me even though
you're nowhere, nothing, dead to all the world —
you interrupt me when I start to talk,
you are the shadow dragging at my heels.
This means I can't step far enough away
to get the thing I want you to explain
in focus, and I can't lean close enough
to hear the words you speak and feel their weight.

Explaining what? What words you speak? What weight?
It's like I said. I can't decide. It's just
that having you suspended all these years
at some clear mid-point between life and death
has made me think you might have felt your way
along the link between the two, and learnt
how one deserves the other. Or does not.

I feel I'm standing on a frozen lake
entranced by someone else below the ice,
a someone who has found out how to breathe
the water and endure the cold and dark.
I tell myself to turn my back. I can't.
I know that what I'm seeing is the guilt
I'd feel if I dismissed you from my mind,
and also know that if I just stay put
and watch the wax-white fingers flop about
I'll start to think they must be beckoning.
I stare and stare and stare and stare and stare.
It's twenty years since you were whisked away,
or twenty-three. That's more than half my life.

Biographical Notes

NINA BAWDEN, born in London, won a scholarship from Ilford County High School to Somerville College, Oxford. She has written most of her life for both adults and children. Among her publications are *A Little Learning*, *Anna Apparent*, *Afternoon of a Good Woman*, *The Peppermint Pig* (winner of the Guardian Prize in 1975), *Familiar Passions*, *Walking Naked*, *The Finding*, *Circles of Deceit* (shortlisted for the 1987 Booker Prize), *The Outside Child* and *Family Money*. She is married to Austen Kark, former managing director of the BBC's External Services. She lives in London and in Greece. Her autobiography *In My Own Time* is published by Virago in October 1994.

MAEVE BINCHY is Irish. She has been a columnist on the *Irish Times* since 1968 and has published many novels and collections of short stories including *Victoria Line* (1980), *Central Line* (1982), *Light a Penny Candle* (1982), *The Lilac Bus* (1984), *The Firefly Summer* (1987), *Silver Wedding* (1989) and *Circle of Friends* (1990). She has had two plays, *The Copper Beech* (1992) and *The Glass Lake* (1994), produced in Dublin.

LUCY ELLMANN, born in America in 1956, has been living in England since the age of thirteen. She is a freelance journalist and has written two novels, *Sweet Desserts* (winner of the 1988 Guardian Fiction Prize), and *Varying Degrees of Hopelessness*. Her father, Richard Ellmann, died in 1987 and her mother, Mary Ellmann, in 1989. They too were both writers.

VALERIE GROVE is British. She was a columnist on the *Evening Standard* and the *Sunday Times* before moving to *The Times*. Previous publications are *Where I Was Young* (as Valerie Jenkins), and *The Compleat Woman*. She is writing a biography of Dodie Smith. She is married, has one son and three daughters, and lives in London.

SHUSHA GUPPY was born in Persia into a traditional family. She went to Paris in her teens to study oriental languages and philosophy at the Sorbonne. Following her marriage to author and explorer Nicholas Guppy, she settled in London in the early 1960s, where she has been living and working ever since. Her marriage is now dissolved and she has two sons.

She is London editor of the American literary journal the *Paris Review* and contributes to a number of publications on both sides of the Atlantic.

She is also a singer and songwriter, and has made twelve LPs of her own and other contemporary songwriters' works, songs by poets, French chansons, and Persian traditional songs and mystic chants. Her new record, *Refugee*, will be released in 1994.

Her first book, *The Blindfold Horse*, won the Yorkshire Post Prize for best non-fiction book; her second, *A Girl in Paris*, was equally well received. Her latest is *Looking Back*, about ten British women writers.

BRUCE KENT was chairman of the Campaign for Nuclear Disarmament from 1987 to 1990, and president of the International Peace Bureau from 1985 to 1992. He was ordained as a priest but left the priesthood to concentrate on the political pursuit of peace. He contested Oxford West and Abingdon for Labour in 1992. His publications include an autobiography, *Undiscovered Ends*, and essays and pamphlets on disarmament, Christianity and peace.

SHEILA MACLEOD was born in 1939 in a village on the Isle of Lewis in the Outer Hebrides. She moved to England when she was five years old and to London when she was six. She was educated at Wycombe Abbey School and Somerville College, Oxford, where she read English and also started to write seriously. She was first published in 1963 with short stories in a Faber & Faber collection of new writers. Since then she has written six novels, including *Axioms*, *The Snow-White Soliloquies* and *The Moving Accident*; two non-fiction books, *The Art of Starvation* (Virago, 1981) and *Lawrence's Men and Women*; two television plays and some journalism. She is divorced, has two grown-up sons and lives in East London.

JEAN MCNEIL was born in Canada in 1968 and now lives in London. Her fiction and poetry have appeared in the Canadian literary magazines *The Fiddlehead*, *Room of One's Own* and *The Antigonish Review*, and in *Passport*, a UK magazine of international writing. She works as a freelance writer and as an editor of fiction, as well as translating from French, Spanish and Portuguese.

PETER MARTIN, born in Brighton in 1944, joined the RAF at fifteen, but preferred writing to mending aeroplanes. Turned down by forty-six provincial newspapers, he got a staff job on *Nova* magazine at the age of twenty-three; he went freelance when he was twenty-seven. He writes chiefly for magazines, most recently in the *Sunday Times* magazine, *Independent* and *Night and Day*.

ANDREW MOTION, poet and biographer, was born in 1952 and brought up in Essex. He has published several collections of poetry, including *Dangerous Play: Selected Poems 1974–1984*, *Love in a Life* and *The Price of Everything*. He has also published critical studies of Philip Larkin and Edward Thomas and two biographies: *The Lamberts* and *Philip Larkin: A Writer's Life*. He has co-edited, with Blake Morrison, *The Penguin Book of Contemporary British Poetry*. His work has received the Arvon/*Observer* Prize, the John Llewellyn Rhys prize, the Somerset Maugham Award and the Dylan Thomas Prize. Most recently he won a Whitbread Prize for his biography of Philip Larkin (1993). He is currently working on a biography of John Keats. He lives in London with his wife and their three children.

DEBORAH MULHEARN was born into a large Catholic family in Liverpool in 1958. She left school at sixteen, worked in theatre wardrobe and travelled abroad before studying English at Liverpool University. After her degree she taught English as a foreign language, sub-edited scientific and engineering journals and then worked for the Architectural Press as a magazine journalist. After the birth of her daughter she returned to Liverpool, where she is now a freelance journalist, writing for local and national publications.

MARY SCOTT is the English author of *Nudists May Be Encountered*, a collection of short fiction, and *Not in Newbury*, a novel. Her stories have been published in magazines and anthologies as well as broadcast on Radio Four. At present she is writing a new novel for Serpent's Tail. She lives in London, where she teaches creative writing, is books editor of *Everywoman* magazine and a regular reviewer for *New Statesman and Society*.

GILLIAN SLOVO was born in South Africa in 1952. She is the daughter of Ruth and Joe Slovo, who were forced into exile in 1964. The family settled in London, where Gillian still lives. Since the birth of her daughter she has been writing full time beginning with three detective novels. She has written two novels about South Africa – the saga *Ties of Blood* and the political thriller *The Betrayal* – as well as *Facade*, set against the London theatrical scene. She has recently returned to crime writing with *Catnap*.

MARY STOTT, born in 1907, is regarded as the doyenne of British women journalists. She was women's editor of the *Guardian* from 1957 to 1972 and still works as a freelance journalist. Her publications include *Ageing for Beginners*, *Before I go . . .*, and, as editor, *Women Talking*.

SALLY VINCENT is a freelance writer. She left school at 16 to work as a reporter on the local newspaper where she served a three year apprenticeship before joining the *Daily Mirror* as its beauty editor. She moved to the *Daily Express* as a feature writer and left Fleet Street after a small altercation at the age of 27. In the course of her freelance career she has contributed to the *Spectator*, *New Society*, *Punch*, *New Statesman*, the *Observer*, the *Independent*, the *Guardian*, the *Sunday Times*, *Today*, the *Evening Standard*, *Nova* and *Cosmopolitan*. She is currently a regular contributor to the *Guardian Magazine* and the *Sunday Times Magazine*.